THE DISAPPEARANCE OF HER MOTHER AFTER HER PARENTS' DIVORCE WHEN SHE WAS JUST FOUR YEARS OLD FILLS DANA WITH A RELENTLESS NEED TO UNCOVER THE TRUTH.

Even when parents divorce, their children are allowed to keep loving both of them.

At least that is how it should be. But shortly after Dana's parents split up, her whole maternal family is cast out of her life. Traumatized but afraid to upset her father, Dana obediently goes along with this plan of erasing the past. Over time, her mother becomes a fading memory, an outline in her imagination, etched in colors. Red hair, white skin, the same blue eyes as Dana's. Unable to voice her yearning to have her mother back, or even to ask questions about her, Dana holds on to proof of her mother's existence wherever she can find it.

In this harrowing memoir, Dana makes her way through her lonely childhood and teenage years, and through her father's second marriage with the woman she is told to call mother. Dana tries to fill the emptiness left by her mother's absence, but she eventually learns that she must harness the courage to face the truth, whether or not that leads her back to her mother.

Editorial Reviews of You-Know-Who

"Family custody stories invariably focus on the dramas surrounding real-time battles over children, the tug-of-war syndrome. But what of the long-term effects? And how those effects shape those same children long into adulthood? In YOU-KNOW-WHO, Dana Laquidara chronicles a different kind of trauma, the time-released microbursts that continue to resonate not for years but for decades. The author's mother was exiled from her life when she was just four years old (and the child's life was "cleaved into before and after," as Laquidara so searingly writes), long before academic and legal studies into Parental Alienation had gained traction. It has taken the author a lifetime to process, to understand, to heal. Her journey is one that she recounts with skill and compassion and boundless love."-- **William J. McGee, author of Half The Child, a novel about child custody and abduction**

"Dana's book is a moving story of alienation from the child's point of view. It is heartbreaking to see her try to make sense of the trauma she was subjected to as a girl. Everyone who works with children of divorce should read this book so they understand why a child may not 'admit' to wanting to see a beloved parent and how loyalty conflicts can last well into adulthood."—**Ginger Gentile, Director of the Erasing Family Documentary and Creator of Reversing Parental Alienation Consulting**

"This book is a must read for anyone interested in understanding the experience of Parental Alienation from the perspective of the child. The author's first-hand account of how manipulation can be used by adults to undeservedly turn a child against a parent they love and intentionally sever familial bonds eliminates any doubt that Parental Alienation is a form of emotional child abuse with life-long impact. I'm grateful this book has been written, because the best chance parents and children affected by alienation have of finding their way back to each other is when those who once had no choice and no voice speak up."—**Doris Newlun, child advocate and targeted parent**

Excerpt

I don't want to leave. When she returns us to our father after each visit, Amy and I sob and scream, both of us hysterical, clinging to her in the driveway. Our father peels us off of her, his words filled with venom. "See what you are putting them through? They are better off without you. If you love them, then let them go." He says this week after week until the snow has long melted and one Sunday when the sun is shining and I don't need a jacket anymore, she doesn't come for us.

YOU-KNOW-WHO

An Alienated Daughter's Memoir

Dana Laquidara

Moonshine Cove Publishing, LLC

Abbeville, South Carolina U.S.A.

Moonshine Cove Edition March 2023

ISBN: 9781952439544

Library of Congress LCCN: 2023903429

© Copyright 2023 by Dana Laquidara

All rights reserved. No part of this book may be reproduced in whole or in part without written permission from the publisher except by reviewers who may quote brief excerpts in connection with a review in a newspaper, magazine or electronic publication; nor may any part of this book be reproduced, stored in a retrieval system or transmitted in any form or by any means electronic, mechanical, photocopying, recording or any other means, without written permission from the publisher.

Cover image courtesy of the author, interior and back cover design by Moonshine Cove staff.

In loving memory of my mother

About the Author

Dana Laquidara believes that creativity, simplifying and healing old wounds are all interwoven; this informs her writing and her life.

Dana's essays have appeared in *The Huffington Post, Literary Mama, Brain, Child Magazine, Boston Mamas, Mothers Always Write,* and elsewhere. She has participated in several Boston Moth storytelling events and took first place while performing a piece from her memoir. She is also the author of *The Uncluttered Mother: Free Up Your Space, Mind & Heart.*

Dana has three daughters, three grandchildren, and resides in Massachusetts with her husband. She can be reached at her website.

https://danalaquidara.com/

PART ONE

I view the happenings of my family as if I were watching a play. I watch so intently that I sometimes forget I am one of them. I am preparing to be the storyteller, allowing it all to percolate inside so that later I can take what I have collected and write it all down.

1
IN THE BEGINNING

If my parents could have seen the wreckage, I think they would have run. If they had known what the future would bring, if they had any idea at all what lay ahead, my parents never would have said hello. They would have run away from that first scene, the one in which they meet, like people avoiding an oncoming train.

My father had a high school football game in the next town over, which happened to be where my mother lived. My mother was at the game with friends and, by some connection, was introduced to my father. They fell hard and fast for each other, a fact I am both thankful for and regretful of; thankful because if they hadn't met, I wouldn't exist. Regretful of the way it unfolded.

I picture them, high school kids, my father, Robert, handsome, tough, hardened by his father's cruelty. And my mother, a sensitive redhead named Jana Ruth Corbin, from a loving, old-fashioned Protestant family.

If asked, I would say that I wish they had just worked things out better. That after conceiving my sister Amy, and then me, I wish that they had been okay enough to skip all the trauma, but I don't think it was possible. I don't think there was any other way for my father and mother to be together in this world, except in tragedy. I have turned their story inside out, wringing it out in the depths of my heart, and it is the only story to tell. The one that was going to be. The one that is.

My mother grew up the oldest of four siblings in the Corbin family. Her brother Doug is a couple years younger than her, then several years later their younger sisters, Lorna and Dara, were born.

I have some early memories of being at my Grandmother and Grandfather Corbin's white cape-style house with its black shutters. There was a barn that housed two horses at the bottom of their backyard hill. My grandparents come to me in the color white. White house, white station wagon, white hair. Their faces faded, but I haven't forgotten their goodness. Being at their home, I was enveloped in love. My doting young aunts, the warmth of my grandparents; I was safe, cared for, loved. Yes, I knew I was lovable then. Amy and I were the light of my mother's life, the precious fruit of her tumultuous marriage. And her family multiplied that love in a way that would never fully leave me.

After the divorce, when I no longer visited my grandparents, whenever I was riding in the back of my father's car I would look out the window and try to find a white house that looked like my grandparents' home. I wanted to believe that one of the houses we passed *was* theirs. I was deep inside myself then, and the mystery of their absence called to my soul, whispering gently, but threatening to expose the darkness that was my grief.

2
ERASED

At barely four years old, my life is cleaved into *before* and *after*. I am standing inside our home with my sister and our young mother. We are wearing our winter coats, and my mother has her hand on the front doorknob. She turns to face my father who has intercepted her, and is demanding to know where she is taking us. We don't go.

When my sister and I awake the next morning, our mother no longer lives with us. This is the *after*.

* * *

"You'll visit your mother on Sundays," my father says from the driver's seat of our blue station wagon. Amy and I are silent. My body tightens and I squeeze my hands into tiny fists and put them under my thighs as if to keep from floating away. I look out the window at the patches of snow in the distance.

We stop at Dairy Queen. I'm surprised that we are getting ice cream in March. As my father gets out of the car, Amy announces that she wants chocolate this time. I'm a little surprised at her request, her boldness, because we never get chocolate. Amy and I always get vanilla. "Okay, chocolate," he says to Amy. I want chocolate too, but I am silent. He comes back with three ice cream cones. Chocolate for Amy and himself, and vanilla for me. I put the cone to my open mouth and feel comforted. The only thing I like more than ice cream is butterscotch sauce. I found it inside our fridge door once, and opened the lid, sticking my index finger as far in as I could, swirling it around and bringing it to my tongue. I could not believe anything could taste so good. Why hadn't my mother told me of this before? Was she hiding it from me? I put it back and scurried away, dizzy with pleasure.

Now I am completely focused on the ice cream cone, as if nothing else in the world exists. When we return home, Amy and I go into our paternal grandparents' apartment downstairs. My grandmother, who we call Memere, wets a face cloth with warm water and washes the ice cream off of my hands and face. Then she makes some comment about how the ice cream will come out of my clothes in the wash. I am amazed that Amy doesn't have ice cream all over herself, too. I wonder how anyone can eat it without getting messy.

* * *

Amy begins having bad headaches that land her in our family practitioner's office. The doctor knows of no cure, but it is suggested that our parents' separation is causing excessive stress that has triggered these headaches. Our maternal grandmother has recently made an offhand comment to Amy about missing us so much that she wants to climb through our bedroom window at night and take us, and now my father is seeing not just our mother, but our entire maternal family as the cause of Amy's anguish and pain. He convinces himself that a clean slate is the best solution to all of it. Our mother and her family would have to go.

* * *

Our mother's apartment is red on the outside. Inside, Amy and I play with the phones, one on the wall in the kitchen and another in the bedroom. They don't actually work, but we pretend to call each other.

She is not the same mother who used to take us sledding and read books to us, not the mother who hosted sleepovers with her little sisters, our aunties. I still see love in her eyes, but I see so much worry, too. Still, being in her presence lets me catch my breath. I don't want to leave. When she returns us to our father after each visit, Amy and I sob and scream, both of us hysterical, clinging to her in the driveway. Our father peels us off of her, his words filled with venom. "See what you are putting them through? They are better off without you. If you love them, then let them go." He says this week after week until the snow has long melted and one Sunday when the sun is shining and I don't need a jacket anymore, she doesn't come for us.

* * *

At the end of the summer, when my father has to return to his job teaching high school, Memere, with the help of Dad's two older sisters who live in town, help care for Amy and me. They help in our transition to No More Mother.

The morning of my sister's first day of kindergarten, as Dad's sister, Aunt Jane, is pulling her hair back into a barrette, Amy bursts into tears. "What will I tell them when they ask where my mother is?" she weeps.

"Don't worry about it," Aunt Jane responds. "If you want, just tell them I'm your mother." Amy gets through whatever awkwardness may have ensued at perhaps being the only child without a parent dropping her off on the first day. Her headaches start to dissipate, but as the days wear on, her Kindergarten teacher begins reporting incidences of her bullying other children.

While Amy is at school developing her reputation as a *bad girl,* I am behaving exceptionally good. I spend many of my days at my father's other sister's home. Aunt Clara's house is just a twenty-minute walk away from where we live, to the end of Cross Street, a right on Broad Street, first right onto Brigham. Most days though, Dad drives me on his way to work, and picks me up on his way home.

During the school day, I sometimes go to lunch with Aunt Clara, sipping sweetened Chinese tea while she chats with her friend. Other days, I walk down the street to Charlie's house. He is a boy my age, and Aunt Clara knows his mother. We play with his toys in his room, or sometimes outdoors. One such day I pee in my underpants and his mother gives me a pair of Charlie's to wear. Later, I am twirling around Aunt Clara's living room in my dress and she notices the boy underwear. It isn't the first time I've had an accident while in Aunt

Clara's care, and I've begun wetting my bed at night as well. Aunt Clara has me pee in a little cup that has a cover and she gives it to Dad when he picks me up. She tells him that he should bring it to the doctor to see if something is wrong with me.

*　*　*

The following year my father remarries and we begin to call his new wife *Mom*. I don't know where my love for my real mother has gone, but I no longer access it. She hasn't just faded into the background of my new life; she is buried beneath it. And with the innocence of a child who had been authentically loved and cherished by my mother up until this point, I still believe I am lovable. I believe my stepmother must be happy to be taking care of me now. I believe this without question until one afternoon when Amy and I are jumping on our beds, singing loudly while strumming toy guitars — *a gift to us, but from who?* — our new mother walks into the room holding scissors, takes the guitars from us, and cuts the strings. The act is so sudden, so violent, that it snaps us into silence.

*　*　*

Dad's new wife happens to be a brunette like my sister, with short, straight hair. My father has dark hair as well. My own hair is lighter, like my mother's, reddish blond, long and curly. I've become the best-behaved little girl, but my hair is still unruly.

One Saturday, we are out doing errands together and a stranger, noticing me with my dark-haired family members, asks, "Where did you get *your* hair?" I don't know how to answer so I stand there frozen, and my stepmother says, "Oh, it runs in the family. She has an aunt with the same hair." Her lie confirms what I already feel; my mother, my *real* mother, must never be mentioned. I want to disappear. I feel shame that my very existence, the sight of me, could blow the family secret.

Shortly afterwards, my stepmother brings me to get my hair cut short. "It is too much trouble to take care of" is the reason she gives to the hairdresser. He is Dad's best friend. The two of them went to high school together and he knew my real mother. Now he is getting acquainted with my new mother, and seems to accept her just like everyone else does. *No one around me seems to have a problem with the fact that my real mother is missing from my life.* It's as if my father is directing a play, and he has simply swapped out one of the main characters, the one known as *Mother,* and the show goes on.

We walk home, New Mother, Amy and I, and it is strange not to feel my hair swinging while I skip along the sidewalk. I run one hand through my new cut, letting my fingers continue down my neck and past my shoulders where my hair used to be.

That night New Mother has made chocolate pudding cake for dessert. As she starts to scoop pieces of the warm cake into dishes, I find myself blurting out, "I don't want any. I don't like it."

"You don't?" She was surprised. So were Amy and Dad.

"I thought you liked it," my father says.

"Yeah, you liked it the other times," Amy pipes in.

"I don't like it anymore."

I watch the rest of them eating the cake that I *do* still like, very much in fact. Saying I don't like it anymore, that I don't want what the rest of them have, somehow makes me feel just the tiniest bit of power. I've made the choice not to eat the cake *because I can.* But the realization of what I've done sinks in as my father goes back for seconds. Now I know I won't be able to have chocolate pudding cake ever again. I hope my new mother will stop making it.

* * *

The morning of my fifth birthday, there is a knock on our door. I am playing on the floor of my bedroom, which is off of the kitchen, and my door is wide open. I hear my father mutter something in a stern tone. When I look up, I see her. My mother is standing in my doorway, holding a box wrapped in pink tissue paper. I catch a glimpse of my father, pacing in the kitchen, jaw clenched. I feel like I am dreaming. I know who she is, this mother of mine, but it isn't safe to love her.

I had momentarily seen her when we ran into her at the toy store in town, just a few days prior. She was with my Aunt Dara and I was with my father, Amy, and our *new* mother. It was a small store and when I saw my real mother, I gasped, wide-eyed. I went toward her until Amy took me by the arm, saying, "Come on, Dana. Come see what Mommy and Daddy are buying you." No doubt Amy had her marching orders and I was whisked away.

Her hair is pulled back in a ponytail, like it was in the toy store, and like it often was when she was *Mommy*. And her face. Do I look at her face? I do, I finally do, and I see love, she is beaming love, but I cannot *feel* it. She wishes me happy birthday, says that she loves me and comments gently on my haircut. Then she hands me the present and watches while I open it. It is a mechanical puppy, brown with a red collar, and when I press a button it walks around, thick and wobbly, pausing to let out an abrupt, high-pitched bark. I keep playing with it, giving it my full attention, pressing the button, watching it walk, picking it up, again and again. I almost forget that my mother is still standing there. *Is she standing there?* I feel dazed, but some part of me is aware that I don't want her to leave. I don't ever want her to leave. But I don't utter a word.

She pokes her head out of my doorway and quietly calls out to Amy who is lingering nearby in the kitchen, while Dad quietly talks to her. When I look up from my new toy, I see Amy turn to face our mother who has stepped out of my bedroom now. In my fog, I can hear them talking. Our mother's voice is full of love, but Amy cuts her off.

"You don't need to come here," I hear Amy say firmly, haughtily. She is only six years old but there is power behind her words. "We have a new mother now. We don't need you."

I don't know if it is a minute later or a half hour later when my mother leaves. I don't remember the goodbye. I just remember that when I come out of my bedroom, no one else is there. Amy has gone downstairs to join New Mother and Dad in Memere's apartment. I don't want to go down there, but like a sleepwalker, I put one foot in front of the other until I have joined them. I don't know what else to do.

Dad, Amy, and Memere are all consoling New Mother who has been crying. She hadn't expected my mother to show up, the *ex*-mother. They have circled her, absorbing her tears. I keep a distance, standing nearby but alone, invisible. I sense a powerlessness that my mind does not allow to travel all the way to my heart, and a dread that my real mother is gone for good. I keep it at bay though; this feels like survival. Stay numb or die. I mustn't love my mother anymore. I put her away. I leave her somewhere within me, somewhere I mustn't go.

I stand there watching *them.* I betray myself with my silence.

***

My screen time has no shortage of wonderful dads who save the day, who get custody, and who help their children see that they will be *quite okay without their mothers, thank you very much.*

The movies and television shows that are chosen for me include, *The Courtship of Eddie's Father*" In this darling series, a widowed father takes care of his young child, a son about my age at the time of my parents' divorce. They are best friends these two, surviving just fine without the child's dead mother, clean and simple. As Eddie's father was courting, so was mine, and soon my sister and I were calling my father's second wife, "Mommy."

In the sitcom *Family Affair,* little orphans Buffy and Jody come to depend on Uncle Bill like a father, their only available parent figure. With my pigtails and freckled nose, I bear a striking resemblance to Buffy and for a time, I adopt the nickname.

With our new mother, we are eagerly taken to see *The Sound of Music,* our first time in a movie theater. As anyone who has seen the movie knows, the von Trapp children gain a wonderful replacement mother, played by Julie Andrews. Once again, the first mother is not spoken of, not once, lest we taint the joyfulness of the father's new life with his now happy children.

My sister and I are *not* allowed to watch *Cinderella.* Even though we see various other Disney movies, the forbidden *Cinderella* includes a stepmother, and a wicked one at that. The word "stepmother" is treated like a bad word, not spoken in our home, not ever, not even through a television set.

Eventually, we are introduced to *The Brady Bunch,* which is popular amongst all the girls our age, and lucky for us, an acceptable option, since the two stepparents, Mike and Carol, simply become "Mom" and "Dad" to their stepchildren. There is no mention of the six children's biological mom and dad, just one big happy blended family without a past.

Lastly, in another handpicked movie, *Kramer vs. Kramer,* the father, played by Dustin Hoffman, takes care of his child after the mother abandoned them both. When she returns to claim her son, there is a fierce custody battle, but in the end, the prize goes to the dear old dad. It is the mother herself, in fact, who declares the dad the better person for the job.

This seems to be a daring act for my father, showing us a movie where the ex-wife and ex-mother actually makes an appearance. I assume he has taken a calculated risk, intending for me to see that I too am best off with my dad.

Instead, though, it triggers grief for my own mother. Once I am in bed, in private, I shed tears. I feel trapped, held hostage to a story that I don't believe.

* * *

Before supper one night, Dad is holding a letter in his hands and pacing the kitchen. He looks up from the letter and tells Amy and me that our grandfather Corbin has died. His words are like air that lift me up, up, out of myself.

How long has it been since I've seen my grandfather? Or my grandmother, my mother, my *other* family? A year? I don't know, really. It was another life, our old life. He was the grandfather of the old me, of *before*. At the age of fifty-three he has died of a heart attack.

Amy and I don't say anything. Our stepmother keeps busy at the stove. Our father still has his teaching clothes on. It looks like he is still working, holding a school paper that he has just read from. *Grandpa Corbin has died.* Now it is time for supper.

* * *

"Lord I am not worthy to receive you but only say the word and I shall be healed." I am seven years old now, and I feel so small as I say these words. *Why,* I wonder. *Why am I not worthy?* What have I done? But my question lingers only for a moment, and then I continue to recite.

Mom and Dad have gone away for the weekend and Memere is taking care of Amy and me. We've come to church with her, St. Mary's on Broad Street. Memere holds her black rosary beads. She recites the words, kneeling and standing and doing whatever she is supposed to do to get into heaven.

We walk home afterwards, and Memere stays outside, talking to a neighbor. I linger with her until I hear Amy calling from inside.

"Dana! Come here!"

I walk into Memere's bedroom where Amy is standing in the narrow space between Memere's bed and her dresser, holding a stack of envelopes, mostly white ones but I see pink and red too.

I stand there taking in the scene and before I can guess what these are and why she has taken them out of Memere's drawer- I know that she has because the drawer is still open; she whisper-yells, "They're cards from Grandma Corbin. And from *You Know Who.*"

We sit on the bed and Amy places the envelopes between us. They are unsealed. Amy tells me it must have been Memere who opened them.

"They're for us," Amy says, an urgency to her voice. She pulls a card out of one and shows me. It's a birthday card for me. Then she opens a Christmas card and reads the letter addressed to both of us. Grandma Corbin hopes we are well, and that we have a good Christmas, she misses us, wishes she could see us.

We are both aware we mustn't get caught. Amy is working fast, but she decides to stop before we've seen them all. She puts the stack neatly back into Memere's drawer and we scurry out into the kitchen. We never tell anyone.

* * *

We don't have a lot of money, but every Christmas morning the living room floor is covered with gifts. My favorite new toy is a doll, and I get lost in my own world playing with it. It is so real to me, this powder-scented plastic baby; I feed it, change it, rock it, put it to bed and then start all over. I take it with me to Aunt Jane's house where we gather for the afternoon and into the evening. I eat too many sweets there, as many as I am able to get away with, and that night I have a belly ache. My father lifts me to the kitchen counter where he gives me medicine or baking soda and water to help me throw up the excess. When I am feeling better, he carries me to bed.

This nurturing side of Dad comes out when I am sick or injured; these are needs he can tolerate. One summer I am sitting on a fence at a bus stop where Amy and I are waiting to be taken to our swimming lessons at the town beach. I fall off of the fence and cut my bare foot on a rock. When the bus arrives, Amy tells the driver what has happened, and after dropping the other kids off at the beach, she drives me home. For the next couple of days, Dad carries me to and from the car when we go anywhere. A neighbor comments on this, on his devotion, his fatherliness. I want to believe this; that he cares for me and wants to protect me. I want to believe he is the hero that others seem to see him as.

I fail my swim test that summer. I have no idea how other kids manage not to sink when performing the dog paddle, or the back float. I am afraid to try very hard; I want to stay safe, my feet in the sand. If feeling safe means failure, then so be it.

We spend many Sundays at Aunt Clara's pool, where I climb in and make my way around the whole perimeter by holding tight to the side. Older cousins try to coax me to let go, to swim, but I refuse. One time, while the adults are enjoying cocktails under the umbrella, Amy picks a fight with me in the water. It turns physical and she keeps pushing me under. I am fighting for every breath, and have no time to holler for help in between plunges. Eventually, she relents and I get out of the water, shaken. I spread my towel on the cement, soaking in the sun for the rest of the afternoon. It feels good to be on solid ground, warm and dry.

3
FIGHTS

I lay still in bed that night. There is always this time between when Amy and I go to bed and before New Mother and Dad go to their room. I listen for their voices downstairs, to be sure they aren't arguing. I know their arguments can turn into big fights and I'm scared of those. So, I listen, and sometimes the voices get louder and I hold my breath but then they are quiet again. When that happens, they are probably just talking to each other from separate rooms, so they have to get a little bit loud. I try to comfort myself.

But tonight I hear the voices getting louder and I can tell they are near each other. It is an angry-loud voice night. I make my breath shallow, and pretend that I can turn down the volume of their anger with my breath. Amy and I don't talk, but we are both listening. We know the other is awake.

Goddamn you! my stepmother says loudly. Then I hear some noise, like somebody is bumping into a wall. My hands are tingling but I don't move them. My heart, pounding. They are in the living room, at the bottom of the stairs. Our door is open a bit because Amy wants it that way at night.

Please stop, please stop, please stop. I chant this to myself over and over. I breath in once after the third *stop*. I breath out only after chanting this three more times.

Please stop, please stop, please stop. Inhale.

Please stop, please stop, please stop. Exhale.

It feels like the game that Amy and I used to play in bed. We sang *the bear went over the mountain, the bear went over the mountain, the bear went over the mountain, to see what he could see.* We had to sing that as many times as we could without taking a breath.

Let me go. Let me get by, you son-of-a-bitch I hear my stepmother saying now. Her voice is loud enough to hear, but she isn't shouting. Then some more noise, like scuffling. Their voices become farther away, in the kitchen, I think. Now it is getting louder and I go under my covers, blocking my ears, chanting, *please stop, please stop, please stop*. Breath in. *Please stop, please stop, please stop*. Breath out.

A door slams. Dad has gone out. Sometimes when he gets back there is more fighting. Other times, it is quiet. Sometimes there are flowers in the morning. I wait for my heart to stop beating so hard. I let myself breathe all the way. After a while I take the covers off my head. I am sweating. I listen for more sounds but don't hear any.

Everything is quiet and then Amy whispers "Goodnight."

"Goodnight," I whisper back.

* * *

Aunt Clara is at the door. My father lets her in and she looks at him accusingly.

"Did you and Meg have a fight? I just saw her walking down Route 9!"

Dad looks away and mumbles something affirmative.

"Go find her and drive her home. She's pregnant for God's sake!" Meg is just a month away from giving birth.

Aunt Clara is firm and my father grabs his keys off the kitchen counter in response. Amy and I go with him.

The three of us ride in silence and then I see her large, protruding belly, quite a way from our home. She is heading to her mother's home which is at least a twenty-minute drive from ours. When Dad pulls over, he tells her to get in the car. She keeps walking.

"Meg, get in the car," he says again.

I am just six years old now, but I can read his tone. *Don't be ridiculous,* it says.

We continue to inch along in the car and he repeats the command again. This time she gets in.

My stepmother rides silently, an air of indignance about her. She must have been furious with my father, I think, to be so desperate to leave. What would she have done once she reached her mother's house? Would she have stayed there? Waited for my father to come pick her up?

Why didn't she take the car? I guess she didn't dare. It was the family car. Dad's car, really, the car that she dropped him off to work in on days she needed to do the grocery shopping. They would wake Amy and me up in the early morning and we'd ride in the back seat in our pajamas.

The truth of the situation is not lost to me. On this day, she is angry enough to want to leave my father. She left without the car because it is not hers to keep. And she left alone, because Amy and I are not hers to keep either. We are Dad's kids.

It is quiet on the way home, other than some attempts at banter coming from my father. He is trying to make light of the situation, to diffuse Meg's anger. I understand this is what he is attempting. She begins to relent.

A chuckle comes from my father. *This is all just Meg being silly,* he conveys without talking. I've become an expert at reading his body language, his facial expressions, the message I am meant to absorb. *Isn't this sort of funny now? Now that New Mother is done with her tantrum, we can all go home.*

* * *

Two years after Baby Julie is born, Dad and New Mother buy a house and in October, we get ready to move. It is only a few towns away, but I feel myself getting further and further from everyone who has ever loved me. I am getting further from *before.*

On my last day of school before we move, my third-grade teacher is saying goodbye and then, more to herself than to me, utters, "It is always the good ones that leave." I know what she means. I am a good girl. I am obedient and quiet. I do what I am told, at school and at home. I am small, impotent, but getting by.

* * *

They still have fights in the new house. This one is the worst one yet. After some really loud yelling, my stepmother tells Amy and me that we are going to walk downtown to her mother's condo. Meg puts Baby Julie in her stroller, and all of us except my father walk to my step-grandmother's home. I think the fight might end there, but then my father shows up and Meg locks the door. He bangs on the door until Meg lets him in. He yells about her leaving the house with everyone but him and then he tries to grab Julie and is saying something about taking her away. Meg is holding on to her tight and yelling for him to go away. Meg's mother moves between them and says firmly, "Give *me* the baby." She says this again, and Meg gives her Julie, who is crying now.

Then our father tells Amy and me to come with him.

Who do you want to go with? Our father demands of us after we get in his car.

We know what he means. He thinks they are going to divorce. There is only one right answer to his question, so our response is automatic. *With you*, we say. We know that we would go with him and Julie would stay with Meg. Just like right now. I feel quite sure he knows it too.

It has been four years since he married Meg, but she doesn't feel like my mother. I know my father wants to believe that he replaced our *before* mother, sort of like a Christmas tree. You just get a new one at Christmas time and forget all about last year's. But mothers aren't like Christmas trees.

* * *

It still feels like summer in late May. I've taken off my school outfit to put shorts on and go outside with Amy. I hang on the high bars of our jungle gym, ignoring the calluses I've gotten on my hands from swinging from bar to bar. Amy sits on a low bar, looking down at the grass. We have both sensed that something is brewing inside the house between Dad and Meg.

Now we hear their voices coming out of the opened windows. I hear their voices escalating. Amy and I try to talk about something-anything other than the panic we are feeling. Then we give up trying. We sit in silence. My stomach hurts.

Meg's scream has turned into a word we can almost make out. She is screaming, really screaming, something that ends in "meeee!"

Then we both hear. "AMY! HELP ME!"

Amy runs toward the house, and I follow behind slowly, feeling sicker now. I can hear my stepmother continue to call my sister's name.

Amy disappears into the house and I can hear her yelling "Stop! Stop it!" By the time I reach the back door there is silence and Amy walks out of the house.

"He had a knife," is all she says as she walks past me and back to the jungle gym.

* * *

There has been a lull in the fighting between my father and stepmother when another one erupts. It starts with the usual tension and raised voices, quickly escalating to shouting. There is some mention by Meg of papers and the words "*She* took them with her." Then a smashing noise, glass, punctuating her words. Meg screams out in pain.

Meg has put her hand through the glass pane of our back door. Since the fighting has morphed into a Meg-is-injured hollering, Amy and I take our places at the scene. Dad is wrapping Meg's bleeding wrist in a kitchen towel, and they are already heading out the door to the hospital, Dad letting out his *everything's okay it's just that Meg pulled another silly stunt* chuckle.

There is glass and blood on the floor, and Amy is quick to begin cleaning it up. I think I should help her, but don't really know what to do, so I just watch. I am stunned that we are left with this, the blood and glass. Amy is efficient in her cleaning up, disposing of the broken glass, wiping up every last speckle of our stepmother's blood. The scene is swept, wiped, disposed of, like it never happened. Like the knife chase, like my mother, my grandparents. What to do with these memories? They are buried in me somewhere, part of me, in my body, my heart. Embers glowing inside of me quietly, I adapt to the burn.

Dad and Meg get home several hours later. Meg is bandaged up and doesn't seem at all upset. It seems she has taken on Dad's version of the incident- she has been silly, ridiculous, how funny that she would injure herself, put her own hand through glass. They are laughing about it now. She needed several stitches and has nearly severed a nerve, but she will be just fine.

4
YOU KNOW WHO

Peculiarly enough, I do not address my entries to 'Dear Diary' or 'Dear God,' but rather to my deceased grandfather.

Dear Grandpa Corbin, I always begin. I somehow feel comforted sharing my thoughts with him simply because he is of another realm, above the confusion and pain of my young girl existence. When Amy grabs my diary from me, in a moment of sibling torment, and reads my entry to our *before* grandfather, she finds it very odd. How can I explain? He is the only dead person I know of, and I think he can be my connection to the divine. And perhaps subconsciously I think, to my mother. I don't know if she is dead or alive, but I know I cannot reach her alone.

* * *

Unlike me, Amy is not so obedient and quiet at home and she gets in trouble with Mom while Dad is at work. Her misbehavior often results in Mom hitting her, spanking her, but mostly slapping her face and arms, her red-faced rage landing where it may. I witness this in silence and then later witness the usual making up, the tearful hugging and kissing and apologies from both of them. I always feel a strange mixture of sickness and relief during the making up sessions.

I typically manage to avoid being hit by Mom or Dad, but I have no choice but to receive Dad's birthday spankings each year. Dad cheerfully says that he likes us to remember who is in charge, no matter how old we are getting. Once we're over his knee, he delivers measured but painful slaps to our behinds. The audience is always the rest of the family, plus Mom's mother who is invited to the birthday celebrations. I find this tradition humiliating and unjust, but refusing to participate doesn't feel like an option. I am alone in my distain, a lone party pooper.

***

As the years pass, every now and then at night in our bedroom, Amy and I whisper about the past. We call our real mother *You-Know-Who* because we don't dare speak her name. She has become a mystery that we are trying to solve by sharing the memories that we have of her. Amy always mentions the affair, and there is disgust in her voice. This makes my heart heavy. Somehow, I know my mother is not bad, but how can I defend her?

"Remember Bob?" Amy asks me.

"Bob who?" I ask.

"You-Know-Who's boyfriend!" Amy answers.

"Oh. Yes. I remember going sledding with him and You-Know-Who."

"Yes!" Amy exclaims, as if I have hit the jackpot. "And that was the day she told us that he was going to be our new daddy!"

"I don't remember that part."

"She did! She said we were going to move away, me, you and Bob, and that he was going to be our new daddy! And I think Dad found out and freaked and that's why they divorced."

"Oh." My stomach flip-flops a little. Maybe she did want us. She was planning on taking us with her, but my father intervened. Why hadn't I known this before? And yet it felt familiar, truthful, this idea that our mother wanted us.

"She had an affair!" Amy whispers forcefully, to make the point again. *Of course* our father would throw her out of our lives for *that,* her tone implies. I can tell my sister thinks we are far better off without her. I am secretly annoyed by her attitude, her stubborn resolve to remain loyal to my father. I feel pretty sure our mother was not just seeking comfort outside her marriage, but seeking a way to escape. She was not only miserable, but afraid. Couldn't Amy see that none of us were able to speak up to our father?

As pathetic as it was, I believed Bob was our mother's escape plan.

"She was having an affair with that Bob!" she repeats, as if I hadn't reacted strongly enough.

"Yeah, I guess you're right."

Did our father really think our mother shouldn't keep us, or did he just want to punish her? New thoughts went racing through my mind.

"She told me she would sleep with me the night she left. She promised me she would and when I woke up, she was gone," Amy says.

I can hear the broken-hearted little girl in Amy. In the dark tonight, I understand why she is so mean sometimes.

"I remember that," I say. "You came back into our bedroom and told me she was going to sleep with you."

I am careful not to breathe too deeply as I say this because it feels like the inhale might pull up the sadness. It is tucked away deep, and who knows what could happen if it comes up.

Other nights we revisit the memory we share of our Uncle Doug, our real mother's brother. *He is big and angry and he is holding our father by the t-shirt, pressing him against the kitchen wall.*

That is all either of us remember, but it fills me with longing. I long to know more. Uncle Doug is the one person I ever saw stand up to my father, contain him, overpower him. I replay the visual over and over, wanting a different ending, a better ending. I want to go back to that moment and let it change everything.

* * *

It is Amy's idea to find our maternal grandmother's phone number and call her up. Through tears, our grandmother tells Amy that our mother has remarried, then divorced again, and has two little boys. She lives in the town she grew up in, in our grandparents' old house. The white house. Our grandmother and aunts live on Cape Cod now; they moved there when my aunts were teens, a few years after we lost contact and after our grandfather died. My grandmother had needed a change she said. After so much grief, it was time to move on. So, she let our mother stay in the white house with her sons, to find her own way forward but with her childhood roof over her head.

Amy decides we will go visit our grandmother and aunts first, and our mother another day. I am surprised by my sister's courage and curiosity. I didn't think she had it in her to go behind Dad's back to find our long-lost family. I didn't think she had any desire to see them again. I agree to go along.

At sixteen, Amy is a month shy of having her driver's license, so she gets her boyfriend to drive us. It requires some intricate lie to tell our parents about our whereabouts that day, but whatever Amy has told them, they believe her, as they usually do. Since high school, she has managed to convince them she is trustworthy, and almost never gets caught in her lies. She came home drunk one night, and I walked her to bed just moments before our parents arrived home from an evening out. I'd simply told them Amy was asleep already, and they never suspected a thing. Once the "bad girl," the naughty one, she is now good. Her anger is reserved only for me. She gets good grades and hangs out with some nice kids. She manages to wear the right clothing, and date a decent guy, and as far as I can tell, her teachers like her. I'm not sure but I think she keeps the truth of our family, our "mother story," from her friends. I think they assume Meg is our biological mother and they comment frequently on how young she looks, how nice she seems, how pretty, and how lucky we are. While Amy seems satisfied that the outside world thinks things are just fine and normal, I feel my spirit shrink every time another person is fooled.

I had been such a good, obedient student through junior high. Now school is requiring more effort of me at a time when I am starting to think that boys and romance have the potential to fulfill me, *save* me. My father is so stern about grades, I don't know why the fear of his wrath does not motivate me to keep my grades up. But somehow, over and over again, I choose daydreaming over studying, both in and out of school. English and Psychology are the only subjects I like, while it feels painful to focus on any of the others. "You know every goddamn word to every song on the radio, but you don't know your history!" my father snaps in the car one day when I am singing along to the radio. While Amy is earning our parents' trust, I am quietly becoming suspect.

So here we are, Amy, her boyfriend and I on our adventure to Cape Cod, with some lie to our parents solidly in place. As long as it is Amy who has devised the whole plan, I don't worry at all about getting caught.

When I get in the car, her boyfriend comments on my outfit. "You're wearing *that* to go see your grandmother for the first time in ten years?" he asks rhetorically. I think he might be joking, but then notice the accusing look on his face. I dismiss it silently, not sure what to think. I'm wearing a pair of light gray corduroys that I like well enough and that fit just right, paired with a flowered blouse. This is the best outfit I can come up with and I sort of like it. And my hair looks good, the curls falling just above my shoulders. Maybe a churchgoer like himself is just used to seeing everyone dressed up on Sundays, I reason. I sit in the back seat, along for the ride, a passenger in my own life.

We arrive at our Aunt Lorna's home first, and Aunt Dara is there as well. They are both young mothers now, and there are a couple of babies around. Amy's boyfriend is whisked away to take a drive and get high with Lorna's husband; two strangers, thrown together under such awkward circumstances.

Amy dives right into her agenda, to voice her anger at our mother, and to seek out validation that we had been terribly wronged by her. I sit flat against the back of the couch, my feet dangling just above the carpet. I look at my knees, study them. I want to fade away. I do fade away.

"She had an affair! I remember him!" Amy says passionately.

Our aunts exchanged glances, and keep their composure.

Lorna calmly offers that our father was not so nice to our mother. She does not
get specific; I sense she is really holding back. It seems like our aunts are trying to protect what innocence we have left, trying not to shake up Amy's emotions with accusations of our father's sins.

Lorna explains that by the time the marriage was dissolving, after that fateful night, she thinks our mother had a nervous breakdown. Amy does not budge in her argument, that Jana was purely guilty of adultery and abandonment, that she, and not our father, is responsible for the outcome. No matter what our aunt gently says in our mother's defense, Amy is not hearing any of it.

"When she came to your house after your father remarried, to see you girls and give Dana a birthday present, you told her to go away," Lorna tells Amy.

"You said you had a new mother and didn't need her anymore. She felt like an intruder, like she was upsetting your new normal. You were confirming what your father wanted her to believe; that now you were better off without her."

Amy resents Lorna bringing this up. She later tells me she felt that our aunts were blaming her for our mother's abandonment. This infuriated her, made her dislike them all the more.

"You two were our baby dolls," Dara says, eyes tearing up. "We loved you both so much. I've never gotten over the loss or the trauma of that time. It was horrible."

I know I had loved them too. Losing them had been part of the collateral damage; everyone connected to our mother had to go.

There is nothing memorable about the goodbye when we leave our aunt's home. I know our aunts are disappointed. They must've been hoping for a pleasant visit, a long-awaited reunion, perhaps some awkwardness at worst. But now it seems there was nothing good about it at all.

It is only a few miles or so to our grandmother's house from there. She is waiting expectantly for us outside.

She greets us as you'd expect a grandmother to greet her grandchildren that she hadn't seen in ten years. She is overjoyed, but cautious not to overwhelm us with her embrace. She comments that I still have my curls and this brings me a twinge of satisfaction, a detour out of my numbness. She has mentioned something in me that was the same as *before*. So much in my life has changed since then, so much left behind, but I know inside there is still that child waiting for someone to come back and get me, wake me up, love me into being again.

We drink lemonade and look at pictures, although I don't really take them in. I am slightly less mute for this visit and Amy has loosened her defensive stance, but she is aloof and I can tell she is eager to get the visit over with.

The table is set for lunch, with enough settings for our aunts to join us, but Amy insists we have to go. Her boyfriend is waiting in his car. We've only been there a very short time, but we say goodbye, and after we are back in the car, our grandmother runs out after us, waving a twenty-dollar bill in her hand. She tells us to use it to buy sandwiches on the way home.

"She's so creepy," Amy says as we drive away.

※ ※ ※

Our aunts told us that Jana's second husband, the man she married about five years ago, turned out to be an alcoholic. When it got to the point where she could not trust him to stay sober enough to take care of their sons if she was out, she divorced him. Struggling to pay the bills as a single mother, she did not have a working phone.

Not having a number to call was just fine with Amy. She'd avoid an awkward phone call and we'd just show up. Within days after Amy getting her license, we borrow our stepmother's car, offering up another lie in order to go see our first mother. And on a Sunday evening, we show up on her doorstep, ten years since we've seen her last.

We park the Chevrolet on the side of the road at dusk, across the street from the white house. Amy's courage wanes this time, and she insists I go myself and knock on the door while she waits by the car. She instructs me to wave her over if someone answers the door. I can hardly believe this demand. This is all her idea and now she wants me to lead the way. I can't even imagine knocking on the door, greeting my mother, this person I barely think of as real. I don't know what I'd say, what I'd do. I would likely be rendered speechless, maybe even faint. But Amy has a way of getting what she wants from me, so inevitably I relent.

Ever so slowly, I make my way across the street. I walk up the driveway and to the side door where a big chunk of the cement step is broken off and lays on the ground. This is the door I've been to so many times as a small child. The step was not broken back then, I think to myself.

I think, but I do not feel. My numbness has silenced my fear, lulling it into submission. I see my hand reach up and knock on the door. I wait. I look across the street at Amy, still standing beside the car, watching me do what she will not do herself.

Several minutes pass. I knock again. What if she is not here? Will I be relieved? Disappointed? I don't know because I cannot feel.

Two heads appear through the glass part of the door. Then they run away, two sets of scampering pajamas. I motion for Amy to come over. If our mother's children, her other children, are home, then she is surely home too. Amy walks closer, but does not meet me at the door. She keeps a distance, making sure that I am the only one in view when the door is opened.

The boys in pajamas have opened it together.

"Come in!," one of the little boys says, excitedly. I glance over at Amy who is finally walking towards me now, and when she reaches me, we both step inside. The boys gleefully run off, leaving us standing in the small kitchen. I look up toward the ceiling where our grandmother's birdcage used to hang. I notice the same light wood cabinets with black hinges that were always there.

"It's Amy and Dana!" one of the boys announces as they both run up the stairs to get their mother, *our mother*. Our mother has been told by our aunts or grandmother that we will likely come visit her someday, and so she has told her sons. The little boys know who we are without us telling them.

Some muffled voices, a door opening and closing, then the boys are back down the stairs, running into the kitchen.

"You can come sit down," the older one says, leading us into the living room and toward a couch. "Mommy's in the bath."

Amy and I sit down on the soft, bluish-gray couch. I think how much smaller the living room looks compared to my memory of it. I recall a Christmas there, playing with a toy at one end of the room, while some family members sit, seemingly so far away, at the other. Now I see that I could probably get from one end of the room to the other in about five Mother-May-I giant steps.

It feels like we sit there endlessly, the little boys, *our brothers,* running up and down the stairs periodically, running through the living room, into the kitchen and back again, looking at us, giggling. We hardly speak to them which is a testament to how *not there* I am, because I adore little kids. I've been babysitting since I was twelve, and I already fantasize about having my own brood someday. I just know I want to be a mother.

But here I am in the home of my real little brothers, and I feel no affection, no desire to know them. No anything.

It's like being in a dream, especially when Jana, *our mother*, finally comes downstairs. She is wearing brown pants and a white shirt, tucked in. It is so ordinary, this outfit. How can a ghost be so ordinary? She is petite like me, with hair and eyes the same color as mine, just as I remembered.

I can tell she is trying not to appear shaken as she offers up hugs. She wipes tears away quickly, telling us that the boys had told her it was us. "I've told them about you and they've been so excited to meet you," she exclaims.

The boys resume their running through the house, up and down the stairs, and through the living room where we now sit. After a little while, Jana tells them to go to bed, but they go upstairs only briefly, reappearing again with laughter. They cause only the mildest of distractions for Amy and me, but Jana stops talking to us every couple of minutes to tell them again they need to go to bed and she will check on them a bit later. I am sure we have upset their bedtime routine, showing up like this.

Amy asks our mother questions, mostly about the affair, and about her abandonment. To my relief, she is less aggressive about it than she was with our aunts. Our mother is kind and gentle, the mother I remember. My *before* mother. I notice her kindness in the way she speaks to us and to her little boys. She calmly, quietly says that our father told her, over and over after the separation, that we were better off without her, and she began to believe him.

"I was weak, afraid," she explains.

"And I just fell apart. I knew your father was determined to win, and I didn't have it in me to fight him. I thought of you girls every day, wondered how you were, if you were sick, if you liked school. I used to drive to your house and park on the street, hoping to see you playing in the driveway or the yard. Once I did see you, Dana. You were on your little bike with the training wheels in the driveway. I didn't dare go to you."

I sit there, silent. I am watching myself, the mute girl, the little sister of Amy, fifteen years old but I may as well be an infant.

I remember an old photograph of me in our driveway, standing next to my bicycle, a five-year old girl. My hair is in a pony tail, and I'm wearing a pink terry cloth short and top outfit. It must have been sometime after she stopped coming to get us, because Dad didn't save any photos from *before*. I briefly imagine this is the day my mother saw me.

"Why didn't you ever come find us later, when we were older?" Amy asks.

"I was afraid to. I was afraid of interfering, upsetting your new life. Afraid of what your father would do."

I know what my father would have done. He would have intervened, simply not allowed it. Had Amy forgotten about the hidden letters she found when we were little girls? There was such a sense of forbiddance when it came to my mother; she was so synonymous with my father's rage that just thinking of her made me anxious.

I wouldn't exactly say that Amy is satisfied with our mother's answers, but she is subdued. I think she at least realizes that this has all been very painful for our mother as well; Jana seems to deflect Amy's anger and accusations simply with her undertone of love and genuineness that is hard to deny. Like that of a mother.

The boys disappear upstairs for the last time, with Jana promising to come tuck them in soon, and she walks us to the door.

"I have always hoped you'd find me," she says.

"I am so, so glad that you did." She hugs us again.

I know we will not be back. I sense Amy will not want to. She will tuck our mother back into the past, not worthy of any more effort, and I will do the same.

***

I have a dream that I am walking, floating actually, up the outside stairwell in our old home, determined to follow my father who is a few steps in front of me. When we get inside, we are both standing in the kitchen, and my father turns to face me. His face changes back and forth from stern to relaxed. When his face is relaxed, it is someone else's face, another, less intimidating man. I reach up and hold his shoulders then, as if to make sure he doesn't turn away. I tell him in a firm voice that I've seen my mother. Then I repeat it, willing myself to use urgency and force. "I HAVE SEEN MY MOTHER. Do you understand that? I went to see her and I know she is real. She is alive and talking and real."

PART TWO

For as long as I can remember, I have been drawn to the mysterious, untouchable, the whisper in the dark, I-know-something-and-feel-it-but-can't-touch-it side of life. Perhaps this was born from the loss of my mother. I remembered the outline of her, like a shadowy figure, unreachable but etched in my memory. She had colors, red hair, white skin, but after a while, no face. I couldn't name her. What would I call her? My mother? My imagination?

5
BOYS: MY DRUG OF CHOICE

I've just turned fifteen at camp, and the sixteen-year-old boy I have become infatuated with has coaxed me out into the woods and put my hand down his pants. *It never occurs to me to say no.*

His name is Tom and it began when my friend Michelle and I were walking in front of him and his friend. I am wearing white athletic shorts and I hear some comment from behind me about my ass.

"He's talking about you," Michelle says and we giggle, turning around to flirt with them.

Tom is instantly mine; I think he is the cutest boy on the planet and I want him for my boyfriend, my first one, right now. We chat for the remainder of the walk and although our words are lacking any substance, in the way of teens meeting for the first time, our mutual attraction is intoxicating. I am feeling happy to be away from home, free in a way that I am hungry for, and now I can hardly believe *this* unexpected good fortune.

Tom and Rick become our camp boyfriends.

We meet up with them at the dining hall later that day, and that evening, the four of us walk to the quaint little New Hampshire downtown. Tom casually takes my hand in his, my first romantic touch. It feels magical; he is magical. And when it is time to say goodnight, still holding my hand, he pulls me away from our friends and under a tree, creating the illusion of privacy. It is my first kiss and a long one; long enough that I wonder how I am supposed to breathe when my mouth is covered by his. I've forgotten about my nose so I am holding my breath. It is awkward and uncomfortable, but I am so, so happy.

The next morning, I pick at my scrambled eggs. Word has spread to my camp friends that I am too lovesick to eat. Tom and I walk hand in hand to the fields, where Michelle and I will play field hockey while the boys attend their next wrestling session. We kiss goodbye, this time quickly, and make plans to meet again for dinner.

Supper is another meal of not eating, spellbound by Tom, his thick arms, his scent, his voice. I love his sixteen-year-old boyish looks, and his confidence. I love his affection and I love that he wants me. Someone *wants me*. When he holds my hand or kisses me, even as I struggle with how to breathe or where to put my hands, I come alive. I escape into this other place that I cannot define. I melt into somewhere else, and I like it. A lot.

The remaining days at camp go on like this, focused on this romance, this new and wonderful world I am now consumed by. Field hockey is secondary, something I do there in body only, while my mind is focused on when I will see Tom next, and what he had said to me last, and how his hand feels intertwined with mine.

The last night of camp Tom wants to take a walk in the woods behind the girls' dorm. In the dark we kiss, longer than the other times, until he motions me to sit on the ground with him. His hands move up my shirt, over my bra, then down to my jeans. He unbuttons and unzips my pants and then his own, all the while his mouth is pressed against mine. I am finally getting the hang of breathing through my nose while we kiss. He takes my hand and places it on his crotch. I've never seen a man's penis before, and although it is dark now, I can feel how large and solid it is. *Hard as a rock*, I say to myself. I am taken aback by what is in my hand, and I don't know what to do with it, so I wait for Tom's next move. How quickly I am going from inexperienced to one of them, I think, the mature girls, the ones who know about sex, who talk about it in hushed conspiratorial voices in study hall, part of a club to which I had not belonged.

I hear some faint voices, muted hollering. They are the voices of camp mates who are looking for me, calling out my name. I scramble to my feet. Tom hears them now too. We quickly collect ourselves without saying a word. It is well past curfew, and I am in trouble. Tom has no such curfew, and we head toward my dorm together, hand in hand at first, until I pull away to run alone.

Two of the camp directors are there, angry, scolding me and threatening to call my parents. My father will be furious at me. Anything but calling home, *please*. They settle on having me pack my bags, and they tell me I cannot participate in the next day's activities, the last day. I am to watch from the side of the field until it is time to go. To my great relief, they don't mention this incident to my father when he comes to pick me up.

I am back home by afternoon and find out that our neighbor, a truck driver, has given us a freezer full of pastries because they are almost at their expiration date. The following day, when no one else is home, I sit on our kitchen counter within reach of the freezer, and I eat one after the other until I am stuffed. The raspberry and cream filling and the flaky crusts are deliciously cold without being frozen. I swear I see my thighs expand beneath my shorts as I mindlessly indulge.

Night after night, I sleep with Tom's red and white t-shirt he has given me to keep, breathing in his scent. I write him letters and eagerly collect the ones he writes back, being careful to get the mail before anyone else. I know my parents would greatly disapprove of my having met this boy at camp. They have strict rules about not dating until I am sixteen, and when I do, they will need to approve. My father will need to approve. Tom, on the other hand, has told his parents about me, and about the night I was in trouble for missing curfew. He writes in his letter that his parents find it hilarious.

I start to tell Amy about Tom, but it feels impossible to disclose the extent of my feelings. When school starts again, Tom and I are still exchanging letters, signing them with love and hearts and promises to stay in touch. He writes about how he'll use his brother's car to come visit me in Massachusetts. At the time, Maine seems so very far away, especially with my parents' strictness creating the greatest divide of all, but I am hopeful that we can make it happen. We can see each other again somehow.

In one of his letters, as an expression of his attraction, he writes that he *loves girls who are small but built well.* I delight in the compliment, and take it as further evidence that we are made for each other. I begin keeping a diary again, writing things such as *Tom and I went to third base* and *I will always be in love with him.*

But by November, Tom's letters have petered out, and although I don't believe there will be anyone else I will fall for as much as I've fallen for him, I want a replacement. I want someone, a boy to call mine, to give my love to and to give me the affection I crave. I need someone to validate my existence.

By December of sophomore year, I begin dating a guy who goes by the nickname Puma. He has already graduated high school and is a friend of my friend's new boyfriend. He is lanky and sullen, with a quick stride that looks part self-conscious and part chip-on-his-shoulder. His light brown hair hangs in his face, and his lips are always pursed, as if holding an invisible cigarette. I am not attracted to him in the least, not anything at all about him, yet I willingly become his girlfriend.

Besides the fact that I am still too young to date according my father's rules, he would not approve of Puma. I don't approve of Puma. He is a heavy drinker. He has no plans to go to college, but he does have plans to enlist in the Marines the following spring.

Other than my friend's boyfriend, Puma does not have any friends. He is a loner who lives with his mother in a little green ranch about a mile and a half from my home. He doesn't know his father, though he must be built like him; his mother is a petite woman, while Puma must be about six feet three. He towers over her. And me.

I have no compass of my own, really. I am lost, my spirit hiding out, while I pile on layers of nothingness. Nothing of value. Nothing true to me. Just experiences that take me nowhere. My mother has been tucked so far back in the recesses of my mind, that I have no clue that it is my connection *to her* that I am seeking.

One night, I am driving around with Puma, sipping from a bottle of wine. Other days, I am spending time at his house, just me and him. He pulls out his guitar, strumming and singing Eagles songs, his deep voice is quiet but forceful, Lying Eyes lyrics pressing out of his skinny lips like a warning.

There ain't no way to hide your lying eyes.

My whole life feels like a lie, one big secret. It feels like I am on the set of a bad movie, no director, no direction. I cannot choose a more honest life because I don't know how to access what is real. *I am not even sure that I am real.* I may be depressed, but not in the usual way that I think of depression. I am not lethargic or hopeless, and I never, ever contemplate hurting myself. And yet, I *am* hurting myself every day. I am just floating mindlessly through life, grasping at anything, or anyone, that might fill this void, a thousand-leagues deep.

My interactions with Puma are devoid of any feeling except uneasiness. Lying in his bed with him, taking my clothes off, I am passive, almost robotic. I am under the mistaken belief that if I awaken my body, I may simultaneously jiggle my spirit free. But I am not setting myself free at all.

Yet I come back, again and again, for no other reason than the wind hasn't changed direction yet. Nothing is pulling me elsewhere.

* * *

One day I am walking home from Puma's house, having told my stepmother I was with a friend. When I am nearing my home, I see Meg standing outside, waving her arm in the air. I think instantly that she must've found out I wasn't at Stacy's house and has been waiting for me. *Did she call there? Did Stacy answer? Or Stacy's mother?*

Damn, I need to think fast. What will I tell her? I am feeling the familiar rush of dread course through me when I notice she has something in the hand she is waving. I want to turn around and never go home, but now my eyes are drawn to this object and my feet follow the curiosity. As I get closer, the dreadful feeling doubles. I feel sick, dizzy, nauseous. My nervous system has gone haywire. She is holding my diary, the green notebook I keep in my desk, in the far corner of my bedroom.

Why did I think it was safe there? It was a simple notebook, the kind you bring to school to take notes in. I had been so stupid to think that desk, that corner, was my own. My stepmother took such little interest in my life, in me, that I simply hadn't imagined her even *thinking* of going through my desk. But I know that is my diary she is holding. I am surer with each tentative, dreadful step.

My diary is my place of purge, my outlet, where I'd been writing since I got back from camp. The words my diary contains race through me now, like bullets I cannot stop.

Tom from camp.

We went to third base.

My father is such an asshole...

The only bad thing I'd left out, and thank God I had, was Puma. I hadn't written in the past couple months, since I'd been seeing him. *Thank God*, I think again, but this brings me only a couple seconds of relief. Even without mention of Puma in my diary, there are enough incriminating words to drive my father to want to nearly kill me, I think.

As I get within ear shot, I hear my stepmother say slowly, through clenched teeth, "Get. Your. Fucking. Ass. In here." *I am exposed. Helpless. They can do anything to me now and I have to bear it, whatever it is.*

My own thoughts belonged to me, but I had made the mistake of putting them down on paper, and it would be a long time before I would want to do that again.

My legs bring me all the way to my stepmother, until her arms swing at me as she tells me she found my diary while looking for scissors in my desk. She offers no excuse for having read it, just the simple statement of how she'd found it.

If only I'd been a braver kid, not so afraid of my father, and of Meg too, if only I'd gotten in touch with my rightful anger, I would have fought back. I would have ripped that diary from Meg's hands and ran with it, or destroyed it before my father ever saw it. And then when Meg came after me, attacking me, not believing I would dare fight her, I would've run, anywhere, to a neighbor, for protection. Or perhaps I would've turned and faced her wrath, hit her back, both our arms flailing and faces red. It might have felt so good, so empowering to finally fight back, fight for what was mine, the right to put my own thoughts about my own sorry-ass teenage life down on paper without it being stolen and being punished for it.

But no, I am not brave. Fear holds me captive.

And then with all of the disgust and venom she can spew, my stepmother says, "After *all* your father has done for you."

There it is. The family story. *My father, the hero, kept me when my mother didn't want me. He sacrificed, burdened himself and his second wife with me and Amy because he was The Good Parent. I should be grateful. I should be good.*

That evening, I sit on my bedroom carpet, arms wrapped around my knees, as my father paces, holding my diary, reading passages of it aloud.

I went to third base with Tom that night.

"We send you to camp and that's what you're doing? Acting like a slut with that *maniac* wrestler!" I know he chose the word *maniac* to emphasize that Tom was from Maine, and therefore somehow a loser.

I'm blinking now, a lot. Twitching. I look straight at him with the most desperate, pleading eyes I can muster. *I'm desperate here, Dad. Please, have some mercy. You've got me and there's nothing left for me to do or say. Let this be over soon. Hit me if you are going to, but just please end this.*

I feel so trapped. I am trapped. I want to die right there. I actually prefer to be dead.

He looks away and reads another line aloud.

"My father is such an asshole."

The interrogation feels torturous, partly because I don't know how it will end. Fear keeps me there. I am compliant. My father is bigger and stronger than me and from experience, memories, and the bulging vein on his forehead, I know I would never get away. Besides, where would I go?

He paces. He reads. He has a belt but he isn't using it. He is angrier and more disappointed in me than he has ever been, so much so that he is eerily calm. He has lost control of me. I dared to do this. I dared to write this. If he unleashes his wrath now, he may lose control of himself. I think he must know this. Or maybe he is just too sad to hit me.

Dad comes to a section that lists my resolutions. I've made a list of things I want to change, to do better. He expresses his approval. "Now here is something good." I am grateful for the respite. I've written something good.

* * *

Bed is my sanctuary. If I could spend my entire existence in bed, I think I would. In bed I can dream and think and be. I dream of falling in love mostly. Of being loved. Of being held. But on this night, lying in bed, I don't fantasize or find peace. Dad has said he will have to think of what my punishment will be. I know this isn't over and that I will have to face him again the next evening. I *have to* make it end. So, I think of a plan.

I decide I will tell my parents that I hadn't actually written all of those words. That someone- I didn't know who, but obviously someone out to get me had to have taken the notebook out of my locker and written in it. They even tried to make it look like my handwriting. And it did! Some of the writing was mine of course, but the worst of it was not. Yes, this is what I would tell them, because I am a desperate girl who would rather die than do more time on my bedroom carpet with my father holding my diary.

And they are apparently desperate too, enough to want to believe I hadn't actually written those terrible things. They believe me. A little reluctantly at first, but then with relief. It gives them an out too. They don't have to face that I really am that depressed sounding slut in the diary who hates her father, hates her home life and wants to run away. They don't have to deal with *me*. And Dad can go back to believing that he is in control.

* * *

Despite having convinced my parents that I was not the actual author of *all* the bad things in my diary, I don't try to convince them that I hadn't written *any* of it. And besides, I think on some gut level they both know the truth, that I wrote every word of it. Yes, I *had* laid in the woods at camp with a boy I met that week. And I *did* call my father an asshole. I *do* want to run away, and I *am*, as evidenced between the lines, in constant search of a romance that will propel me out of my miserable state. Although gut level is not a place that either of my parents hang out in, I know the truth must have leaked through their denial at least enough to make them suspicious of me. I have to be extra vigilant now.

* * *

It is springtime and Puma is leaving for the Marines boot camp. We agree to stay together, but I don't mean it. I feel neutral at his leaving, or possibly relieved. He cries, and utters promises to write to me as much as possible and call me when he can, and to come back to me on his break. He talks about someday being together always, and talks about this separation as something sad but temporary. I nod in agreement, affirming all that he has said, knowing that the chasm between his expectations and mine is a problem that I will deal with once he is gone.

Within a couple of months of Puma's departure, I have a blind date with another friend of a friend's boyfriend. My friend Stacy shares with me that this guy, named Brian, is very good-looking, but rumor has it he has a less than stellar history with girls.

I am sixteen now, and therefore legal to date, by my parents' rules. Stacy, her boyfriend, and Brian pick me up at my house, an hour before the wrestling event we will be attending in Boston.

I sit in the backseat with Brian, and I am in agreement with Stacy that he is good-looking, but I am completely unsure of what he thinks. Does he think I'm pretty? Is he disappointed? The four of us drink beer as we ride, and carry on some sort of group conversation, but Brian and I do not exchange a single word. We steal glances of each other in the backseat, but do not make eye contact.

Neither Stacy nor I are interested in the wrestling match, but the guys are fully engaged, enthused. At one point, Brian passionately raises his arms in the air in a sudden, sharp motion, and whacks me on the side of the face with his elbow.

"I'm so sorry! Are you all right?" These are the first words he's spoken to me and I am thankful for the interaction.

I let him know that yes, I am fine. He seems genuinely sorry, caring. It is ironic that an accidental physical assault makes me see him as gentle.

When we leave Boston, I am in the backseat again with Brian. About ten minutes into the ride, he abruptly pulls me to him and starts making out with me.

The four of us arrive at Brian's house late into the evening, and his parents either aren't home or they are in bed. Brian flicks some lights on by the pool, and then he seems to materialize more beer out of nowhere. We sit drinking in the lounge chairs and then the two guys end up chasing each other around the pool, hurling beer and obscenities.

When I stand up from my chair to go pee, Brian appears by my side and sweeps me up into his arms. He resumes his running, full speed, around the pool while threatening to throw me in. My fear is not of getting wet, but of getting hurt. I know he has had several beers at this point, and I am terrified he is going to fall and drop me on the cement. I plead with him to stop running, the only words I have spoken to him all evening, but he keeps going. Stacey yells at him, but he is undeterred. Stacey's boyfriend laughs.

Brian keeps running, laughing and shouting wildly, until he tires himself out. I am so relieved, so giddy with relief when he finally puts me down. I run back to my chair and sit breathless, waiting for my heartbeat to slow down to normal. Stacy puts her arm around me and I laugh with tears in my eyes.

* * *

One evening, Puma and I have a scheduled phone call at seven o'clock. I know I don't want to see him again, and I think that breaking up with him over phone, long distance, will be the quickest and easiest way to let him know. I sit waiting in my bedroom with my hand on the receiver. At 7:05 the phone rings and my heart leaps a little with fear. Hearing his deep, serious voice reinforces my decision, and I get right to the point.

"This isn't going to work. We are going in separate directions, and we need to end this."

I knew he'd be very upset, but I'm not prepared for the sounds that come through the phone. He swears and hollers and cries. The distance, the fact that he cannot get to me, that I will not have to see him, keeps me from panicking. I remain calm and just keep repeating that it isn't going to work and this is what I need to do. There is no consoling him, and in fact his outrage is only escalating, so I hang up the phone. I stand there, knowing what is coming next. The phone rings. I hang up two more times, without speaking. He gives up.

A few weeks after I thought my break-up mission was accomplished, I get another call from Puma. He informs me that he has been discharged from the Marines and is now home. I hang up as soon as I can, willing him not to call back, but of course he does. Again and again. I keep answering the phone because I fear my parents picking it up. I make up some excuse of why a friend is suddenly calling for me so much. I ask Puma to stop calling, but he is angry and persistent. This goes on all weekend. *What happened to Once a Marine always a Marine?* During the last of these calls, he demands that I return the large stuffed lion he had given to me.

Desperate to end his calls, I seize my opportunity when my parents are out for the afternoon. I jump on my bike with the huge stuffed animal under one arm, steering, unsteadily, with my other arm. I can hear his guitar before I reach his house. Upon seeing him sitting on his front step, I quickly get off my bike and walk toward him only as close as necessary, and throw the lion on his front lawn. He stops strumming long enough to curse at me. I get back on my bike, heart pumping, legs pumping, and go home. I hope this will be the end. I don't know what else I can do to be rid of him, but I know if he keeps this up, eventually my father will find out I've dated him and I shudder to think of that.

A few nights later, Amy wakes me from a sound sleep.

"Dana, Puma is outside!"

At first, I think I'm dreaming. Then I think it's a joke, a terrible one. I hadn't filled Amy in on what I'd been going through with Puma. I thought that confiding in her might increase the chance of our parents finding out. Or at best, it would result in her telling me if I had followed Dad's dating rules, I wouldn't be in this position. And it's true, I wouldn't. I know that dating Puma was a horrible choice, and I am sure that she thinks so too.

I sit up and blink hard. Amy is at the window. I am not dreaming. I hear music. Loud music.

"Look out the window! He's right there."

Shit. Shit. Shit. It's true.

There he is with his portable music player, or boom box as we call it, howling something unrecognizable. I sit frozen, helpless, terrified our parents will awaken.

Amy and I sit in disbelief, her more amused than frightened. After several agonizing minutes, he tires of his antics, and the music fades away as he walks off into the night.

Dad and Meg's bedroom is at the opposite end of the house, and whether they haven't heard the serenade or they've simply brushed it off as something next door, the next morning they don't mention anything. I eventually find out through a friend that Pumas was arrested that night for disturbing the peace. I don't hear from him again.

* * *

The following winter, my father and Meg go away for a weekend and they take Meg's car, the only one I am allowed to drive. This leaves me with no transportation for getting to my waitressing job on Sunday. I don't want to lose this job and I don't have anyone that I feel I can call for a ride.

Out of desperation, I call Puma because I think he will want to see me, and therefore be willing to drive me both ways. He arrives at my house early, somehow eager and aloof at the same time. I try to make pleasant talk in the car but he is in no mood for chitchat. When we arrive at the restaurant, the giant parking lot is icy and he spins his steering wheel recklessly, losing control of his car in the wide-open space of the parking lot. I am terrified and I beg him to stop but he is enjoying this. My pleading seems to egg him on, so I become silent, waiting it out.

I think he just may not value his own life all that much, let alone mine, and so I am not sure if I am waiting for him to stop doing donuts, or waiting to die.

He stops. My God, he stops.

I get out of the car, knowing as I walk away that I will ride home with him later. I don't feel I have another choice.

* * *

I am not a big drinker, but I'm invited to meet up with a few other girls before a school dance, and one of them has managed to score a couple bottles of wine. I don't know my limit, and by the time we get to the dance, I am visibly drunk. There is always a policeman monitoring these events, and a sober friend recognizes that I may get in trouble for my inebriation. She kindly insists on walking me home, and knowing we will have to walk past the policeman standing by the exit, she comes up with a plan. She tells me that we will pretend I am upset and she will keep her arm around me as she comforts me, but really, she will be using her arm to steady my staggering gait.

Her plan seems to work, as no one stops us as we walk out into the night air. My friend keeps her arm around me, walking slowly, steadying me, until we reach my house. My parents had been out for the evening, but as luck would have it, they are home earlier than I had expected. I will have to get myself to bed as quickly as possible, hopefully without them seeing me first.

It is all I can do to walk in a semi-straight line through the door when my parents appear in the kitchen. They know within thirty seconds that I am drunk. My father tells me to sit down in a chair that he has now placed against the wall. He pulls off his belt, and begins to rant and rave at me, pacing back and forth, occasionally snapping his belt against the wall. From the window, he had seen the girl walk me home in the dark, a tall girl with short hair, and he is convinced it was a boy. From a distance, arms linked, it appeared that we were a couple. This has increased the level of my offense ten-fold. Not only am I drunk, but he thinks I've gotten drunk with a boy. I cannot convince him otherwise. In the midst of his fury, he punches me in my left arm, just below the shoulder.

I feel the blow, but in my numb state, it isn't such a big deal. I mean, the anticipation of being hit feels worse; once the blow lands, it's almost a relief. Then I am dismissed to bed where I fall into a fitful sleep.

When the bruise appears the next day, large and purple, it is impossible not to notice it in my short-sleeved blouse. My stepmother's eyes widen when she sees it and before she can comment, Dad mutters, "That was probably from me."

I think I hear a tinge of regret in his voice. His rage has been made visible.

6
FIRST COMES LOVE

The summer before I begin college, I am working in a research library doing various odd jobs like filing and photocopying. An avid reader, I thought I'd like working in a library, but this one is filled only with technical books which hold no appeal to me. Books, books, everywhere and not a one to read. I am bored to death with the job, the environment. Until I meet him.

Carl appears fairly regularly now in the research library. He comes over from his lab to use a book or two, always making a point to make eye contact and say hello. On one particular day, he approaches me and asks me out.

"Do you want to go out on a date, sometime? Maybe dinner or a movie?"

I am struck by how direct he is, how unflinching. I hesitate and into my long pause he inserts, "It's okay if the answer is no. I can handle it."

"Maybe you could ask me later?" Then feeling like I need to add clarity to this odd request of mine, I tell him that I am on the verge of breaking up with my current boyfriend.

Two years my senior, my boyfriend, Jimmy, is working as a roofer. He will only meet my father's standards if he has college plans, so I've been pestering him about taking classes. Perhaps he will want to run his own roofing business someday and would need a business degree, or a math degree? He could start with just one course. That would enable me to tell my father that he is working toward a degree. I am relentless, but why? I don't even think I am love with Jimmy. Before I have even accepted him myself, I am expending my energy trying to make him into someone my father will approve of. We date for nearly a year, and although I want to pretend that ours could be a serious relationship, we both know it is not. In fact, it is destined to end soon and seems to have become only a matter of which one of us will declare it over.

"Okay, sure," Carl responds. "So, later as in later today, or later this week, or in a month?"

I am feeling self-conscious about the openness of this exchange. The library is silent except for this guy asking me for a date, and me fumbling for an answer. I'm not sure how many people are within earshot for this exchange, but as a minimum, my work friend is witnessing the whole thing. This doesn't seem to affect Carl in the least.

"Next week," I answer.

"Okay," and with this answer, he leaves.

He comes back the following Monday, a week later, and having officially broken up with Jimmy by then, I say yes to a date for that Friday, after work.

When my father hears about my date with Carl, he walks into my bedroom, demanding to know if Jimmy knows about it. He hadn't gotten the word that Jimmy and I had broken up. In that moment I instinctively know I have triggered his residual anger at my mother. In my mind, he may as well come out and say it. *I think you are acting like your mother and I despise your mother. I despise her so much that I have erased her from your life entirely. You look like her and that is troubling enough. I will not let you become like her; lacking ambition, pregnant, a cheater. Worthless.*

* * *

My first date, and every date thereafter with Carl is calm. I feel safe in a way that feels like a great relief, familiar to my soul. By now I know that in theory, the correct thing to do is to focus on myself, growing up, healing and finding my own way in life, not dating another guy. And yet I feel deeply that I have come home, and I want to stay.

I am stunned by how comfortable Carl is with his parents. I mean, he is like an adult, talking to two other adults, as if they are equal human beings. And they *like* each other. It is so entirely different from my experience and I can tell he takes it for granted, not in a bad way but in a way that he's never imagined anything else. He has no idea how much I envy this. But just as Carl chooses to love me, so do his parents, and eventually I start to believe that I am worthy of it.

* * *

When I turn eighteen, my father tells Amy and me that Meg will now legally adopt us. There is some murmur about how it will simplify things for the future, when we apply for a marriage license and need to put our mother's name on the application, for instance. The reason for waiting until I've turned eighteen is an obvious one; there will be no need to contact our real mother, who is in fact still our legal mother. Once I am eighteen, I am free to be adopted if I so choose. Or in this case, if my father chooses. He proudly and happily declares we will do this, and so we do.

I feel sickened by this. At eighteen, it would have felt so much more natural to distance myself from this family and its secrets. Instead, in some cold, dimly lit office in Boston, I sign my name to the façade and then we all go home and have cake. I hate this day. I silently hate it.

Amy hates it too, but for a different reason. She says she feels that Meg was already our mother, fully and truly. This piece of paper is hardly necessary, a formality not worth talking about. To be legally adopted by our stepmother means we weren't officially her kids until now and Amy doesn't like to think of it that way.

Our father is the only one celebrating. He gives Meg a stuffed teddy bear and a card. He wants her to feel special, joyous. He probably wishes Amy and I would make her feel special too, but we don't.

* * *

When I first tell Carl that Meg is not my real mother, I do so matter-of-factly, and without many details at all, the same way I've told friends. And when I ask him to come to the courthouse with me, to look up my parents' divorce records, he agrees. I don't know what I'll find, if anything, but I am eager for information, for tangible clues.

There is a wall of drawers, alphabetical by last name of divorcees. I find my parents' file and in it is a sealed letter addressed to my mother at her parents' address. Scrawled across the address in black pen are these words: *Return to Sender. Whereabouts unknown.*

I glance around the courthouse and there is absolutely nobody paying any attention to us. I open the envelope and inside is a piece of paper stating that my father had been awarded temporary custody. It is signed by his lawyer.

The following week I borrow my stepmother's car to visit Memere. I haven't seen her in a long while and I feel a bit sad about this. I pick her up and we go to her favorite department store, poking through racks of random clothing on sale. Neither of us buys anything, and then we cross the parking lot to have lunch at Friendly's.

Memere orders a grilled cheese and I get a clam roll. Before our food arrives, I find myself bringing up the subject of You-Know-Who and I wonder if this was my intention of visiting Memere all along. I don't recall ever talking about my mother with her before and yet I know that I can. Just like me, I doubt she would ever bring the topic up to my father. I think she is intimidated by my him, at least around this topic, and what she says confirms this.

She tells me that on the court date that was to determine custody, my father had instructed her to pack a suitcase for Amy and me. He told her that if our mother showed up and gained custody, he was taking us to Canada right away. We had relatives living there, and they'd give us a place to stay, at least temporarily. Memere would need to keep this a secret of course, if it came down to this.

I can tell by the way Mems talks freely about my mother, that she assumes I share the same "us against her" mentality. Everyone must assume that. Why wouldn't they? I've gone along. I called Meg "Mom." I kept quiet. I played the role of the abandoned daughter just fine. I belonged to Dad's tribe. But inside I knew, I just *knew*, that things weren't as they seemed. There was more to the story, more than just what my father wanted any of us to know.

"She asked to borrow some towels and then she gave them back bleached," Memere tells me.

Well damn. Thank God she has been banished from my life. I mean, who would want a mother who could bleach someone else's towels? Sarcasm plays in my head as I silently take in Memere's words. Then I begin to laugh and it's hard to stop. She must assume I'm laughing about the towels, really finding the story hilarious.

But truly I have no idea why I'm laughing, and I have little control over it. Memere doesn't seem fazed by it though. She probably just thinks I am being silly, childish; although I am eighteen, in her eyes I *am* a child. But I'm a child she can confide in. She can tell me about my bad mother. There is more.

Memere tells me how our mother left Amy and me with her boyfriend's friend one evening, while she went driving around with her boyfriend. We had been tucked away in bed, and our father was working late, possibly at his bartending job. Watching from her window, Memere had seen who came into our apartment and who had left. Then she sat in the stairwell, outside our door, ears perked, until our mother got home.

The guys were from Fort Devens, a nearby Army Reserve Base. *Couldn't her boyfriend have come alone and just hung out at home with my mother? I mean it looks extra bad to leave us alone with a stranger, assuming my mother hardly knew the friend. I know they would have had to pass background checks to enter the army reserves, but still. What if he was drunk, irresponsible, or worse, a child molester without a record?*

It occurs to me how ridiculous it is that I am wondering about this. I mean, am I so desperate to get inside my mother's mind that I am fixating on her lies and what she could've done differently, better? To not get caught?

Then I wonder just how long this affair had gone on before my father found out; before the big bad night, the night that marked my before and after lives. The night of no more mother, the devastating blow to my psyche that I will probably spend the rest of my life adapting to or trying to fix or undo – or what? What did I need to do? At eighteen, I have barely begun to ask that question. I am still just gathering the clues, but for now the truth feels like the most important thing.

I remember a comment Meg made to someone on the phone when she didn't know I was listening. She was talking about my mother and said, "Oh she did it again. She walked out on another family, another couple of kids and a husband." I suspect she got this information from Memere or one of Dad's sisters, but I don't know. Like many false rumors, there was one piece of truth. Yes, she had divorced again, but she had custody of her two sons. I was silently outraged by Meg's total acceptance of hearsay as fact. She must have been so satisfied hearing this false story, one that validated the story of my mother that my father had already given her; that our mother just left. She just leaves her kids. That is what she does.

I had swallowed my outrage back then, as usual, after overhearing my stepmother's phone call. Was it only my fear of my stepmother and father's reactions that kept me from speaking my truth and instead letting it silently chip away at my spirit? Or was it also fear that full acknowledgement of my feelings would make me come undone?

*　*　*

By the time I leave for college, Julie has become very sullen. She runs track at her high school, and my father is a passionate fan. He critiques and cheers and doles out more attention with this activity than I've ever seen him give anyone. Julie is a good runner and track becomes increasingly important to her. Around this same time, a neighborhood girl her same age comments to her on Meg not being the mother of Amy and me. This is traumatic for Julie; no one in our family has ever spoken about this to her. *No one.*

I am actually surprised the neighbor even knows, since it is such a taboo topic amongst my family members. If Julie has done the math, and she probably has, she already knew that if Meg were Amy's real mother, she would've given birth to her at sixteen. So, Julie either thought this was the case, or she knew there was another truth and was simply afraid to ask questions; but she surely hadn't expected the truth to come out of the blue from a neighbor. I imagine her shock and humiliation; she likely had no idea how to respond. Whatever the details, the encounter troubled Julie a great deal, and when I am home from college on a break, it is obvious how upset she's become. She calls Meg from school, crying, unable to make it through the day. She feels betrayed, lied to by omission, haunted by this topic that is a dark cloud over our family.

All the while, my father and Meg have an air of annoyance about this. She isn't even a child of divorce, they reason, why is *she* so upset over it? They have no idea how to address Julie's emotional pain, so they handle it by being offended.

I witness Julie's desperation, her turmoil, as well as our parents' exasperation. I feel helpless and guilty. *Why hadn't Amy and I ever addressed the topic with her? Why didn't I ever talk to my baby sister about it?*

* * *

My college years go by in a blur of classes, friends, waitressing, and visits from Carl. He continues to make me feel wanted, and loved. Our relationship is comforting, grounding, and some sound part of me urges me to hang on to it. When he sees me put a cigarette in my mouth that I am handed at a party, and he yanks it out with urgency, I don't protest. He pulls me to his side and then moves me forward.

It feels like he is always moving me forward, toward somewhere better than where I am.

So, when Carl graduates from college and tells me that he wants to join the Air Force in order to become a pilot, and asks what I think of this and will I join him after I graduate, I said yes. Yes, I'll come with him and yes, I think he should follow his dream. I know that I can barely run my own life; I certainly don't want the responsibility of holding someone else back. Besides, I would go anywhere with him.

We are engaged by the end of my junior year and he has been accepted into the Air Force as a pilot-in-training. I take a heavy load of classes at the start of senior year in order to finish a semester early, and before Christmastime, we get married.

The morning after our wedding, having breakfast in our hotel, I think *This is my husband. I am his wife. I am important to someone. I matter.*

I am elated.

I leave for Texas with Carl on New Year's Day and when Amy expresses sadness at how easily I can go, I don't know what to say. It is true. It is so easy for me to go.

But once I have moved, I find it stressful to navigate my relationship with Dad. I try to call home as often as I think is expected of me, but not too much because I get the sense he and my stepmother are relieved to have me grown and gone. Does Dad feel obligated to put Meg on the phone when I call, even if she'd rather not talk? Would he rather not talk? Trying to take my father's emotional temperature is much more difficult now that I am long-distance.

During the weekdays, I am kept busy with my new teaching job. But in my spare time, a feeling of doom has begun to make its way to my consciousness. I talk with Carl about this icky feeling I am having and how I think it is related to my family-of-origin. He agrees that it probably can't hurt to see a psychologist on base, and it's even free to me due to our military benefits.

I have just one appointment with this guy. I try to describe my feeling and I suggest that perhaps it is partly homesickness, although I know it isn't that, not really. But I do feel sick, or at least mildly depressed, and I am pretty sure it has something to do with home.

Sitting in the black leather chair, I tell him that I feel bad, guilty perhaps, after speaking to my father over the phone. I can't quite gauge what he is feeling, or wanting, I explain, and it leaves me very anxious.

He tells me that this is fairly normal. "When we are far away from loved ones, we may imagine that things are not good, we may worry more. Perhaps you need to come right out and ask how he is doing."

I know he isn't quite understanding me. This isn't *it*, this isn't the problem, but do I even know myself what *it* is? I take a gamble that I do know what it is, and I put it out there, matter-of-factly, without emotion. I figure if he is to help me, he should have the information.

"My parents were divorced when I was four and I stopped seeing my mother shortly after that. We don't talk about it."

My words hang in the air, but not for long.

"It does us no good to rehash the past and find things to blame our parents for," he says.

It feels like a slap. I am ashamed, shut down. I don't go back.

I walk home, and before going inside, I look up into the sky. *Please God*, I pray. *I don't know what to do. Please help me. Help my family.*

* * *

Our first daughter is born in Texas, with so much red hair that even strangers can't help but comment. Carl and I are thrilled to be parents, and although we are muddling through the newness of it all, we take to it well.

Amy has also recently had a baby girl, and Dad calls our baby daughters his "twins."

He and Meg fly out to visit, and greet us excitedly when we pick them up at the airport with our firstborn in tow. An early riser, my father gets up with her in the wee hours of the morning and feeds her a bottle of breastmilk that I've left in the fridge.

When our baby girl is almost a year old, Carl is finished with his Air Force commitment and gets hired by a major airline. We have had enough of the military lifestyle and are eager to buy our own home as soon as we can, back in the Northeast where there are trees and winding roads and a sky that is interrupted by hills.

* * *

We are back in Massachusetts and I am pregnant with our second daughter when I finally reach out to my mother. I am ready to hear her story now. I *want* to hear her story. She responds to my request right away, and we make plans to meet up at a mall, half way between our separate lives.

It is a warm September day and my mother leans out of her black Ford Mustang to wave to me. She still recognizes me, I think. She parks her car and meets me at the main entrance of the mall where I've been waiting, having arrived early. As she walks towards me, I think she looks young for her forty-seven years. Her hair is still reddish and long and her body is small. When she gets closer though, I see the lines on her face and the tiredness in her eyes.

We walk together through the mall, looking for a place to sit and talk. We barely glance at each other as we make small talk. Here we are, two women with such similar features, obviously related, and yet we are strangers. We keep walking until I suggest we turn around and go back to a restaurant we just passed.

As we sit down, I look at my mother curiously. I want to absorb every detail of her appearance. She is wearing a copper-colored lipstick that looks good against her fair skin. Her dark blue eyes are just as I remembered. I had only one photograph of her which I hid from my father, knowing he had discarded the others. She is far away in the picture, in the background, but I was thankful to have found it. It was in an old bureau in our basement, and it proved to me that she was real.

It feels surreal to see her again. I wonder how I will begin to ask all of the questions I had waited so long to ask. But then she just starts talking, explaining everything. After a while, she stops fighting the tears. I listen to her story.

My mother speaks of her marriage with my father and how much it eroded her self-esteem. "Your father got his college degree and bragged about his educated friends. The way he treated me... I absorbed it all and I began to feel worthless and unappreciated."

She describes instances of abuse, though she does not call it that. "It didn't happen every time we fought," she says, after telling me of her broken wrist.

She tells me about her affair with the man that promised to take her away from my father.

"Your father found a letter from him and threw me out of the house that night. It was the middle of winter and I wasn't even wearing a coat. I couldn't face my parents, so I spent the night with my boyfriend. I intended on coming back to get you girls, but your father had gotten temporary custody by the next morning. His lawyer called it abandonment." Now the letter at the courthouse makes sense.

Her shame kept her from asking her own parents for help. They thought it very important, as the mother of two children, that she stay married. But did they mean *no matter what?*

I picture my mother, hiding out with her lover, while my sister and I stayed at home with our raging father, not knowing if she'd be back.

"After that I had visitations with you on Sundays," she continued. "You and your sister cried so much when you had to leave me. Your father told me it was too hard on you both. He told me over and over again that you were better off without me. I began to believe him. I didn't fight for custody. I didn't have it in me to fight your father. I just broke down. I was dying inside." By the time my father remarried, the Sunday visits with our mother had stopped. "You girls were everything to me. The sadness, and the anger I had at your father, I can't begin to tell you.

When Jana was done talking, I stared at my glass, nervously stirring the ice with my straw. I was convinced that my mother really had loved me. I believed her, had known it all along. But somehow facing it felt devastating. The stranger I once called "Mommy" wasn't "You-Know-Who" anymore. She was a real human being who had suffered a huge loss of her own. She was sitting across from me, breathing, talking, crying.

"I became the best-behaved little girl because I sensed that was all the adults around me could tolerate," I told my mother. "When my own needs might have caused them any inconvenience or distress, I kept them to myself. I don't ever remember mentioning you to my father, let alone grieving you. I went into a state of melancholy that others just accepted as my quiet nature." I surprise myself with my own honesty. But I can't allow Jana to believe that her absence had not damaged my life.

So, I tell her of the void in my life as I grew up without her—the loneliness, the confusion and shame. She averts her eyes, as if she can't stand to know how much pain her absence caused me. She needs to believe that I had been okay.

Jana walks me back to my car. After an awkward moment, she puts her arms around me. She feels small, her grip almost frail. She is weak after all. Too weak to fight for me. Too weak to stand up to my father. She left him, but I never got away.

We parted, not knowing where we'd go from here. No tidy, happy ending to our story.

7
The Stranger I Call Mother

My emotions start surfacing, like an iceberg breaking up, and I am furious at my father, so much so that I fear what I will say or do if faced with him. My grief over all the lost years with my mother, the years stolen, overwhelms me. My mother has confirmed for me what I have known all along about her absence from my life; it shouldn't have been. She did love me. My sister and I were weapons my father used to punish her. It never made sense to me that the parent who I felt loved me most of all was the one to disappear. My kind, loving mother. All the senseless suffering, the cruelty. My father hated my mother far more than he loved me, that felt certain.

I cry for days, to Carl and by myself, but I do not confront my father. I stay clear of him for weeks, then a month or more and he doesn't seem to notice.

One day I glance up at the black and white framed photo of Amy and me when we were toddlers. I am smiling in the picture, hair curly and wispy, not at all indicative of the thickness it would gain later. Amy looks serious, almost pouting, big brown eyes with hair cut into a pixie. This photo had been tucked away, making it large and looming, inside a hutch in our childhood home. It was the only photo of our babyhood that we had ever seen, a forbidden reminder of the *before* days, when we were our mother's children.

But after Amy had her first baby and was careful about photographing even the smallest of milestones, she began complaining about not having any baby pictures of herself. So, my father made copies of the photograph and framed them, he and Meg presenting them to Amy and me. I was surprised by this gesture at the time, knowing it was a big step for them, bringing that time period out into the light of day like that. But Amy was a force to be reckoned with, and I knew my father wanted to placate her. I sensed pride in his presentation of this gift, or maybe it was relief. The *lack of photos* issue was put to rest.

※ ※ ※

I know I need some help processing my feelings, so I begin therapy with a kind, older man named Dr. Johnson. I tell him my whole story, and this very act of truth-telling causes me to have a panic attack when I go home. I don't know what is happening, just that my heart is pounding and I am having trouble breathing. Once the tingling in my hands has settled down enough to make a call, I reach out to him. I am relieved that he can assure me that I am not losing my mind or dying.

My subsequent appointments with Dr. Johnson are less anxiety-provoking, now that I've gotten my deep dark secret out of the way. I start to feel a bit less shame and fear, and more curiosity and comfort.

I begin to have dreams that feel significant. In one dream, I am a child, barefoot and sitting in his office, legs dangling from the chair. In another dream, I'm a child again, but this time I am outdoors, running around in the grass, happy, under a sunny sky. Then I suddenly have a choice to turn a corner, but the horror of what would be around the proverbial corner in my mind feels like more than I can stand, so I don't. I share this dream with Dr. Johnson, and he thinks that it is a 'before and after' of losing my mother, which makes complete sense to me. If the psychological stress of my mother-loss was more than I could handle in real life, as a young child, what did I do to avoid "turning that corner"? I am genuinely curious, and also deeply sad for my child-self for the first time in my life.

Dr. Johnson urges me to have a conversation with my father. He does his best to hide his frustration at the fact that my father has not been confronted, by me or anyone else. He says he thinks I am afraid to express myself because I saw the price my mother paid; however recklessly she expressed dissatisfaction with her marriage, she did, and then she disappeared. He also thinks that every moment I spend with her from now on will be healing for both of us.

He has given two assignments, without calling them that. The first one, talking to my father, feels impossible. Intellectually, I know that I am capable of opening my mouth and uttering my mother's name to my father. I know I won't die or even get hit. I'm an adult, one with love and support in my life. I *should* be able to do this. But the psychological block around discussing the past with my father feels so real, so impenetrable, that I don't even consider trying. I nod my head and let my therapist think I agree with him, that I ought to do it. And I'm not lying, because I do in fact agree with him. I agree I ought to do it. But I know I won't, at least not yet. And the other assignment, spending time with my mother, feels only slightly less scary.

* * *

Our second daughter is born in the middle of a snowy winter, and I am content to hibernate inside our happy home with my growing family. My mother and I have been writing back and forth, and the following summer we meet up at a family reunion hosted by my grandmother's sister at her lake house. My grandmother, aunts, uncle, brothers and mother all in one place, welcoming me and my family. Everyone comments on how much my mother and I look alike. Our oldest daughter is almost three now and the baby is eight months. My mother seems delighted to have two granddaughters, and so happy that her mother and her sons can be part of this reconnecting too. My brothers are teenagers now, and I wonder if they remember the day Amy and I showed up at their home when they were little. I envy their uninterrupted relationship with our mother.

I am glad I went to the reunion but I also feel deeply guilty, or shameful, like I am doing something wrong. Like *I* am wrong. This doesn't make logical sense to me, but it feels involuntary, as if my mind has been infected and although I know the virus doesn't belong there, I don't know how to get rid of it.

I reach out to my mother a few weeks later, to try to figure out when we will see each other again. It will require some prioritizing. She is a single mother of two teens, working full time as a nurse's assistant and I am the mother of two small children. We live an hour and a half apart. It seems we are both thrilled and terrified to be reconnecting. Dr. Johnson would be pleased if he knew, but I have stopped our therapy sessions. I am navigating this without him.

I've shared the bare minimum with Amy and it seems she is both curious and uncomfortable. I talk to Carl more, but I don't invite his thoughts on it. I don't want anyone pressuring me to stay in touch with my mother or challenging my fear. I need to stay in control of where this may or may not be headed.

Jana and I continue to write each other letters. It is a slow way of communicating, but it is steady. I ask many questions about the past. I save all of her letters, stuffing them in a manilla envelope one by one until I can no longer close the metal clasp.

Dear Dana,

All the years that I wasn't with you and Amy on your birthdays, I've always wanted to get you something special to remember me by. I don't really know your likes or dislikes yet, so I just went by my taste. I hope you like this ring. I had such a good time shopping for a birthday gift for you. All the other years I just dreamed about it. Rubies are my birthstone, too, so I thought this would be nice for you. You're very special, Dana. I love you.

I'm glad you went to the reunion. I'm sure you must have been nervous! Everyone was so glad to see you and the children and to meet Carl too.

I bet the kids slept on the way home. They had a busy day. They are so good and what a couple of cuties. You have a wonderful birthday. We'll be thinking of you.

Love,
Jana

P.S. If you think of it will you send me Amy's address so I can write to her. Thanks!

Dear Dana,

Just a short note to let you know I work the weekend of the 22nd but during the week would be fine. Also, there's a boat parade I think the last weekend (Sunday) at the lake.

I wrote Amy a letter. I had started to write to her a few times and just broke down. It took me two hours to finally finish the letter tonight. I feel drained, angry, and very sad rehashing everything again. I don't know if I'll hear from her, but I'm here if she chooses to get in touch. I certainly don't want to force myself on her.

I sent Amy a couple of pictures with the letter, and here is one of you. Look at that hair!

I have a feeling we're a lot alike even though you were with your father.

I'll call you soon.

I hope the girls are doing well. Can't wait to see you all again.

Love,
Jana

One day my father drops by unannounced to see the kids and say hello. I direct my daughters to greet him and they thank him shyly for the candy bar he hands each of them. When he is saying goodbye, giving me a hug, he says, "Do you know this is my little girl? I am her daddy." And without missing a beat, one of my daughters says, "And Mommy has two mamas!"

I know my father is stunned, and I am too, but he forces a chuckle. *Silly child.*

I know if my mother is back in my life, I will either have to tell my father or keep it a secret from him and I find both of these options unacceptable. I don't yet have the courage for the first option and the second one just seems so wrong. What message would that be sending my children? What burden would I be placing on my own children by asking them to keep such a secret? Or what reaction might they get from my father or stepmother if they innocently revealed the truth? Shock? Distain? I cannot set them up for that. For now, my father probably just assumes I've told my kids about my mother. That is different from actually inviting her into our lives. I begin to share my dilemma with my mother in my letters to her. I need her to understand how "impossible" this situation feels to me. And I continue to ask more questions about the past.

Dear Dana,

I've been waiting over two weeks for some slides of you and Amy to be made into pictures. As of today, they hadn't come in, so I'm sending what I do have to you.

How are the children? I bet the baby is getting big already.

I love the pictures that you sent. I was on my way to my sister Dara's shop so I opened my mail at her place. She thinks it's great that we are keeping in touch. And of course, she and I had a good cry for ourselves after talking about the situation!

I hope with all my heart that we can have a relationship where we can at least get to know each other.

If I had been the one to get in touch with you first, would you have told your father? I don't see why he would worry about me being in your life, now that you are an adult, except that he may worry about your feelings towards him for not mentioning me. He may have felt that by you not asking questions when you got older, that you weren't interested or curious. I can't imagine why he wouldn't be understanding now if you and Amy wanted to see me.

I have three (four now? Did Amy have her 2nd baby yet?) beautiful grandchildren and the thought of not being able to see them and know them because they might say something in front of the wrong person is really breaking my heart. How does this end?

Love,
Jana

Dear Dana,

Got your letter and photos yesterday. The girls are getting so grown up. I can't believe how big the baby is. She looks like your brother Rory. My mother thought the same thing.

You were a good baby. You were very happy. As you got a little older, you were still happy, but pretty quiet. I felt extremely close to you. Your father's family always seemed to make such a big deal over Amy, probably because she looked like his family. But your father's sisters would always tease her though until she'd get so mad. Then your father would punish her for getting mad!! Many times, I remember him making her go to her room and stand in the corner. You just seemed to look afraid.

I believe you walked before you were a year old and you talked very young. Amy was such a chatter box that I'm sure you learned from her. I spent a lot of time with you both, reading and singing to you.

I'm sure you heard your father and I fighting. I know I never yelled back. I don't remember you ever seeing Rob hit me. Whenever he would yell at me, I would either have you in bed or have you play in your room.

It's only been the last three years, after counseling that I've been able to stick up for myself verbally. All through my adult life I've been attracted to controlling men. It started with your father controlling me, and now I worry he is controlling you.

Kris is starting Cape Cod College Sept. 5. He's also working for me at the nursing home doing floor care. Rory is working at a Mexican restaurant in Falmouth. Right now they are both looking for a rental with a friend. They are still with me right now, though.

I met Paul a couple months ago. A few girlfriends took me out to celebrate my new job, he knew who Dara was and he asked me to dance. We went out to dinner the next night, started walking most evenings and have been dating ever since. He's been divorced (2nd time) for twelve years. He has daughters 30, 29 and a son 27 and five grandchildren. We go out dancing (which I love to do). We go out to eat and other things. We have a lot in common. Paul is a contractor and builder and is building a house on Cape Cod. It should be done by October.

I'm anxious about your essay being published. I'm sure it will be. I also think writing about your feelings helps the soul, too. I'm very proud of you, Dana.

How's Carl? How's his job? Well, let me know when you hear from the magazine.

Love,
Jana

My mother has touched upon a painful truth. My father is controlling me, or rather *I am allowing how I believe he will feel about this reunion* to influence me. But I need my mother to understand for how long and how deeply I have been influenced by *what my father wants.* I am seething over her ignorance of this. She experienced my father's control and abuse; did she really think his personality wouldn't affect me?

You're the one who left me with him! I scrawl in my next letter to her.

Without her understanding of how difficult it is for me to stand up to my father, I don't see how I can welcome her into my life, a life that was very much built on her absence. Her early fear of my father, and letting him convince her of her own unworthiness, cost me my childhood. It cost me my mother. And now she expects *me* to be bold and confront him.

And how can she focus on romance when we are trying to rekindle our mother-daughter relationship after so many years apart? Why isn't she calling me more, initiating getting together, bending over backwards to make sure we spend time together? Why doesn't she get it that it will take a Herculean effort on her part to get to me to face my father on the fact that we are reuniting? I need her to burst forth in my life with such force and confidence as to leave me no choice but to tell my father. I need her to show me that she believes she is worthy this time; that she loves me enough to do what it takes.

At the same time, I need her to know why she can't just burst forth and why I can't let my father know about us.

It is dangerously tempting for me to declare her unworthy of this reunion. If she hints at being the bad mother whom I was expected to believe she was, then I don't have to do anything. I don't have to face my father. If she is that mother who cares more about men than her own children, then I can keep living the life I am living, no courage required.

In my next letter, I point out what I perceive to be her mistakes, how she is screwing up our chances at connection. I write to my phantom mother, instead of to the real person that she is. I give in to the relief of pushing her away. Then I await her response.

Dear Dana,

Happy Birthday! I was planning to call you today to tell you that, but I received your letter in today's mail and decided against calling you.

I guess I've been going about things the wrong way. I've been letting you do most of the contact. I felt that was what you would want and I didn't want to make you feel like I was pushing myself at you. By doing that I believe you think I don't care. I would call you every day if I could, just to let you know that I'm thinking of you.

Dana, I know there is no reason or explanation for me not being there for you and Amy. I wasn't a fighter then, I let people walk over me. Through fear, insecurity, and being intimidated, I eventually came to believe that you and Amy were better off with your father. That is what he wanted me to believe and it was wrong. I can't change things, and I can't undo things, Dana. If I could cut off my arm or leg to prove to you both that I didn't leave you and stay away because I didn't love and miss you, I would!

I do know and understand your pain, believe me. I have gone through all these years wondering about school, whether you were sick, wondering every day what you were doing. I have grandchildren, Dana, that I may never know. You and Amy have brothers that are grown up now.

I don't know what the answer is for us. If it makes you feel better to blame me and hate me, it's okay. I've hated myself for years for not fighting for you and Amy and standing up to your father.

You and Amy were my whole world. I was a good mother and loved you both more than anyone could. It was because I loved you so much, I thought your life would be better without me. Your father made sure I felt very little of myself back then and that I would leave you both alone if I really loved you and Amy. I have a lot of bitter feelings toward him still.

All the love that I had over twenty years ago for you and Amy is still inside me. I'm sorry you couldn't have known that when you were growing up. I'm so proud of how you both turned out, and I wish you all the happy things you deserve.

I had gotten pictures together of members of my side of "your" family. I was going to put them in a small album and send it to you. I was all excited while I was getting them together, but then I felt again that I may be being too pushy, so I never sent it.

I hope you have a Happy B-day, Dana. For every birthday that you and Amy have had I've had a good cry for myself on that day because I couldn't be with you or tell you how much I love you. Well, I'm crying today, but at least I can tell you (whether you believe me or not) that I love you, Dana.

You mentioned that you didn't write the feelings you have to make me feel guilty. I'm sure I felt some guilt because I didn't fight your father. But I was made to feel from the beginning of when your dad threw me out, that if I loved you and Amy that I would get out of your lives, that it was best for you. That was drilled into me over and over. With you calling your step-mother "mommy" whenever I visited, I let myself be convinced it probably was best. I was wrong. I'm sorry. You can never know how much.

Love,
Jana

My mother has mentioned harboring bitter feelings toward my father and I wonder how she hasn't expressed them to him at any point in time. Is she still afraid of him? I fantasize about her facing him once and for all, telling him what she thinks of his past actions. But I also wouldn't want to be blamed for "setting her off."

I muster up the will to send my father an email. I know the only way I can salvage a relationship with my mother is if it is out in the open. I cannot live with secrets and fear any longer. I talk with Carl, and with his help, I draft an email. Then I sugar coat it just enough to be able to send it.

Hi, Dad,

It is not at all my intention to stir up bad feelings, but impossible to address this w/out doing so. Also, I have always known Mom's feelings in this matter were a major concern to you. I do not feel the need to mention this topic to her.

I had a recent visit w/ my grandmother Corbin. I have also spoken many times with Jana and asked many questions. The answers that I got during these talks, combined with my own memories, eventually brought me some peace of mind. I remember being close to my mother and her extended family. It was a relief to learn that my mother did not simply and easily leave out of lack of love, which is what I think you expected me to believe.

While growing up, I sensed it would be too upsetting to ask you questions, or say how I felt about all ties being severed, and about pretending my mother for the first four and a half years of my life never existed. I did not want to hurt anyone else's feelings, make anyone angry, or disrupt the status quo. But the arrangement never felt normal to me. As much as you'd wanted to simply replace my mother, and her family, it could not be done. So, I eventually went about figuring out how to gain some understanding and healing on my own.

It has taken me many, many years to get up the courage to bring this up to you. I am taking the chance now of being forthcoming. I appreciate your willingness to answer questions or explain past actions. However, I am not interested in blaming or judging you or Jana for what caused the breakup of your marriage when you were both quite young. It was the aftermath that was most painful to me. I do not say this out of a need for pity. I say this only because I cannot be free or have peace until I say my own truth.

I appreciate you opening up to this painful topic. If you do not wish to hear another word about it, I will certainly respect your wishes. If you want to respond to this, I will listen. But the last thing I want is for us to argue over whether my own feelings are 'right' or not. My feelings are just a natural outgrowth of a past I had little control over.

Love,
Dana

I nearly have to leave my body to press send. I have to suppress all emotion, and just let my finger hit the button. But as soon as I do press send, I am flooded with an anxiety I can no longer contain.

Two days later, Amy calls me and she is angry. *She has spoken to Dad, and he is distraught. He feels sad, accused, worried that my maternal family has turned me against him. He is shocked I would bring this topic up after all these years, and he just doesn't know what to do. He didn't mean to put her in the middle, but she could tell something was really bothering him so she probed.* She tells me all of this with urgency, and she wants me to reach back out and make things better.

"I've told Dad he can reach out to you, too. I think if you two talk, I should be there. I can help you straighten this out. You should've heard Dad. He is so upset, Dana."

I am not surprised that Amy is his spokesperson. He gave her that job when she was just five years old. "We don't need you here," she had said to our mother, and she carried that distortion with her into adulthood. The truth is, we did need our mother. Of course we did. She has had the weight of that myth on her shoulders nearly her entire life. Now I am trying to correct the narrative, and she is trying to get me back in line. Our father *needs* me back in line, and in a way, so does she.

I defend myself. I call her an enabler, brainwashed. I tell her she has been psychologically abused, manipulated, and that her denial is hurting us both. Thirty years of emotion makes its way out of my body in a fit of words, messy and disjointed. She attacks me back until we are both spent and we hang up.

The following day my father requests by email that we get together. We meet for lunch and before we go in to the restaurant, he tells me his story, defending why it was necessary for my mother to be exiled.

"I loved her. I don't know what she told you about why she was unhappy, but maybe I wasn't around enough, didn't pay enough attention to her."

I feel he is trying to find out what I know, if I know about the abuse. I don't tell him. I just listen.

"I never told you bad things about her before, I never spoke badly about her, but now I feel like you are forcing me to. She had affairs. I forgave her for the first one, but then she did it a second time. What kind of lifestyle would you girls have if you lived with her? I had nightmares, terrible nightmares about not seeing you again. I don't know how much you remember about that time, but I hope not much. It was very painful."

When I think of how completely and abruptly my bond with my mother was severed, I want access to the pain that I felt as a little child, traumatized and grief stricken. To *not* feel it now, to not know exactly *what I felt, how I suffered* — it is that *not* knowing that drives me mad. Is the pain still within me? I want to get it out. Out of my body, out of my heart.

Tell me, Dad, I want to say. *Tell me please, did I go to my room and cry? Did I dare to ask for my mother? Did I look to you for comfort? What did I say? When did my tears stop?*

"I had better never see Jana," my father says now. I am taken aback by the sharp flash of anger that appears in his eyes, and the familiar locking of his jaw that I hadn't seen for many years. He essentially killed off my mother's children, and *he* is still angry at *her*?

"And your *mother* would be so hurt to ever hear about this conversation." He emphasizes the word *mother* and I know he means my stepmother.

He had been talking as the victim, doing his best to elicit my sympathy, my understanding of why he had to "protect me" from my real mother. But now he is offering me a warning. His demeanor has changed. Rage still active. Noted.

My old programming kicks in and all I want in this moment is to soothe my father. Even as I know I am in psychological servitude to him, I don't stop it. I shake my head. "No, you won't run into Jana and Mom won't hear about this," I say.

My father reaches out to embrace me. "Are we good now?" he asks, smiling. I accept the hug and he says, "I hope we never have to talk about this again." We go inside for lunch. He tells me about his work project, his latest exercise routine, his diet. He asks about my children and expresses his pride.

I am playing my old familiar role again, and as inauthentic as it feels, it soothes me too.

* * *

In hindsight, talking to my father should've just steered me back to my mother, but instead I take my need for truth seeking in another direction. I ask my mother what her ex-lover Bob's last name is and to my surprise, she not only remembers and answers me, but she does not ask for any explanation as to why I want to know.

About a month goes by before I follow up on the lead and I am able to narrow my search to two possible Bobs. I leave the same message on both their answering machines- "I am looking for Bob who was at Fort Devens in Massachusetts in 1970. If you could be so kind as to call me back, I will explain." It turns out the Bob living in Colorado is the one I am looking for. He calls me back the next day, hesitant and perplexed, but also curious to know what I want. I quickly tell him I am not a long-lost-daughter, or any relative, but that I think he knew my mother, Jana Corbin, back in 1970. Upon hearing her name, he immediately remembers her.

I tell him that I am searching for answers, for memories, to try to piece my story together, to try to better understand my mother and her choices, and perhaps gain more insight into my parents' marriage and its demise. Unsure how much Jana had shared with him about the fateful night that my father found his letter, I briefly fill him in and remind him, lest he'd forgotten, that she spent that night at Fort Devens. I tell him she never returned home after that night.

He says he had lost all touch with my mother shortly after that time, and that he didn't know about the divorce, but that when she visited him at Fort Devan's, she was often upset due to her rocky marriage.

He sounds intrigued now, flattered that my mother had thought of him, like he is barely trying to restrain his excitement over this. He mentions his fiancé being home at the moment, and that he has fond memories of my mother, but little detail to give after such a long, long time. Before we hang up, he gives me the phone number to the store he works at, and asks me to call him anytime; he's happy to follow up soon with any further information that surfaces in his memory.

The next day he calls me, eager to talk again. "I remember more," he proudly announces, talking more openly now, from the privacy of his quiet store. "Your mother was the sweetest, prettiest thing, and I wish I could've done more to help her. It's breaking my heart that I couldn't do more at the time. You and your sister were precious, and I would've been proud to call myself your daddy if I could have." I interrupt him now, suspecting he has been drinking, and beginning to regret ever contacting him. Something in his voice, in addition to the intoxication, sounded desperate and felt invasive. I felt a desire to get him back out of my life, to reverse the clock and undo this contact.

"I had and still have a father," I say. "I would not have expected anything from you." Whatever his choices, my father was still my father. I am annoyed now at Bob's ignorance, his drunkenness, and the way he speaks of my mother like she is purely innocent in all of this.

"Please don't ever blame your mother for any of this," he says. "My heart is just breaking. It's been forty years and now all the feelings are flooding me."

Oh God, I've opened the floodgates of this old man, this guy who now thinks my mother is sitting around thinking of him after all this time, and that perhaps they should've been together.

"Couldn't I just give your mother a call?" he asks, hopefully. "It would probably trigger more memories, and then I would report back to you."

"No. I cannot give her phone number to you. I barely have contact with her myself and I am not going to be discussing this with her."

"I just want to say hello, and I promise I will tell you everything that is said."

"Absolutely not."

"Oh please."

"No. I have all the information I need now. I am all set. Goodbye."

The next day another call. I am about to hang up on him, but he says something that, despite not wanting it to, has caught my interest. "There's something more. Your mother did not stay with me the night your father threw her out. She had started dating another guy by then, someone higher in the ranks than me at Fort Devens. He had permission to leave the base, and he picked her up. I believe he snuck her into his room and that's where she stayed that night. His name was Randy Groton.

"She was dating someone else?" I asked, perplexed and yet not shocked.

"Yes."

Now I realized, if he was telling the truth, it was probably not even *his* letter my father had found, but the letter of her other, newer lover. In essence, I had tracked down the wrong guy.

Now my father's story of catching my mother not once, but twice in affairs, made sense. I had already believed him, but this shed more truth for me. Bob was her lover, but not the last one she planned to run away with.

And now I had no interest in finding the other guy. I had heard enough. It just didn't matter anymore what the other guy would be able to tell me, if anything, about my parents' marriage, or my mother's emotional state, or anything else.

My mother was right to be afraid to ask for a divorce from my father. That is undeniable to me. Instead, she fantasized about escaping with the help of a man, and if it didn't work out with one man, try another.

I want to get Bob out of my life, out of my business, and return to my present life.

I want to wipe away the contamination of my past.

8
A Lifetime of Words

By the time our third daughter is born, I have justified pushing my mother away. When I tell Amy that it isn't working out for us to reconnect, her response is "See, Dana. She doesn't *want* you!" My sister believes I have proven her right.

I have convinced myself that I am doing my best and choosing the most peaceful path. I am enjoying motherhood, busy with my own family, steeped in love. I am moving on from the past and living life in the present. And a few years later, when my mother moves to Arizona with her boyfriend, and my brothers follow, I choke back my regret.

One ordinary Sunday I am saying goodnight to my oldest daughter and I linger extra-long because she seems sad. She cannot pinpoint what is bothering her, and so I just sit with her, stroking her long red hair.

"It feels like someone is missing," she says finally, almost in a whisper.

I take a deep breath and fight off the feeling of despair that threatens to overcome me. She adores her two younger sisters who are surely asleep by now. Carl is a wonderful father to our girls. We both love them more than anything. Yet she feels someone is missing. I want to assure her that no one is missing, that we are all here and we love her very much. But I also don't want to discount the feeling that she has articulated.

I wonder if the missing "someone" is God. Once Catholics, we had stopped going to church several years ago, jumped right off the moving sidewalk of sacraments before her Confirmation. I had encouraged our children to pray and nurture their inner lives, not wanting to throw the baby out with the bathwater, so to speak, but my encouragement was weak and inconsistent. I mostly thought if we loved them well, they would grow up trusting themselves and their own intuition.

And maybe this is what is happening; my sensitive daughter *is* trusting herself and she is intuiting that someone is missing from her life. From our lives. I let the thought arise within me, the thought that I really don't want to have. I allow the *possibility* that she is missing my mother too. What if she is embodying my mother wound, inheriting it? What if all my daughters do?

* * *

Two thousand five hundred and ninety-two miles. That's the distance between my home and where my mother lives now, near the southern border of Arizona. Two thousand five hundred and ninety-two miles and eight years; the distance between then and now, between the day I last saw her in Massachusetts, and now. Today we are further apart than ever.

I think of the harsh words I used to keep her away *eight years ago*. The words I cannot take back. The time I cannot take back.

My mother works hard and cares for her many pets and lives out her days with a boyfriend; I hear he's mean.

In this time, I've continued to have a strong marriage, and to be the mother I always wanted to be. I am the mother now, but I am still the alienated daughter, too. I thought I could forget that and still be whole. I thought I could live as if my mother doesn't exist. But my daughter is right; someone is missing.

* * *

I write a letter because it feels safe. I have time to choose my words carefully, so very carefully this time. Besides, I'm not sure that my mother is ready to hear the sound of my voice again. I keep my letter brief, mostly asking how she is doing. Finally, for the first time, I really, truly care how my mother is doing. For the first time since I was four years old, I am letting myself love my mother. I *want* to love my mother. I keep reaching out by letter and I tuck her responses in my top bureau drawer, pulling them out now and then to reread, looking for clues that there is still hope for us, looking for clues of forgiveness.

Dear Dana,

Thank you for the letter! How are you and Carl and the children? I'm sure the kids are really growing up. I've wondered how everything has been with you. I had felt a strong connection between us when we had gotten in touch years ago and you had come to the family reunion. I had hoped that you would get to know your brothers too. Kris got married two years ago. He and his wife are living in in Mesa, AZ. They are very happy together.

I don't even know what to say to you anymore. There has always been a huge hole in my heart since you and Amy were gone from my life. I've just gone along feeling this was how it is and not expecting anything different. I know I should have done things differently all those years ago. I can't change the past. God knows I wish I could. I love you and Amy so much and I hope that someday you will both at least forgive me for not being there for you. Please take care of yourself.

Love,
Jana

Hi, Dana,

Just got home from work. I work Mon-Fri, mostly 3-10 at an assisted living home. I've always enjoyed the elderly. My place of work now is a 5-bedroom home. I have filled in on weekends a couple of times, but prefer not to. I've always had to work at least one weekend day the last 14 years, so having weekends off is new to me!

My mother will be out to visit. She doesn't mind traveling as long as it's not by plane. Sure, I will include Kris and Rory's addresses. I'm sure they would like to hear from you. They didn't say much when we didn't hear from you again. Just that they thought you were going to keep in touch. I know they were both excited that they had a sister that they would get to know. They remembered the time you and Amy came to the house in Hudson years ago. I can't help but cry as I write because of all the years that have been wasted that we could have been getting to know one another.

There is a lot that we need to catch up on. Is there a good time to call you or would you rather just write for now?

Love,
Jana

Hi Dana

I called the other day (Mon) but got your answering machine. Had hoped to call Tues but was away all a.m. and then worked until 12 a.m.. I talked to Rory yesterday. He said he received your letter and would probably write back. I remember when we had reunited and he knew he had nieces, he was so excited that he was an uncle. He thought that he would get to know them, and you and Carl, but then it didn't work out. I think he was quite hurt by it all and said that you didn't know him and Kris and didn't want to. I hope he does write. I think it would do him good to be in touch with you. He's a very sensitive guy and takes everything to heart. Well, I will close for now. Hope to catch you this weekend by telephone.

Love,
Jana

Dana,

Thank you for the photos! Would it be okay to start sending them gifts on b-days, etc.? I keep remembering when I used to send you and Amy gifts and your grandmother (Memere) hid them. If you feel I shouldn't send gifts, that's okay. I will understand. They don't even know me and I don't want you to have them keep any secrets from

Rob...Thank you again for the pictures. Now at least I have faces...They have grown so much! I will show them to Kris and Rory.

Love,
Jana

Dana,

I brought my 14 yr. old cat (Tux) out here. Also, two dogs from an animal shelter and 2 parrots. I love animals! More than a lot of people! One of the dogs (Mindy) reached out from behind her cage at the shelter and cried when I went to donate some comforters. I was not looking for a dog. I went back two weeks later, and she was still there...crying and reaching out to me. I adopted her that day. The other dog (Boston) I adopted as a puppy for Rory. He is the sweetest dog. When Rory moved to an apt a year ago last May he wasn't able to have any pets. I LOVE this dog so I've kept him with me. Oh, also got 2 baby chicks 2 weeks ago at the Bisbee Farmers Market. As for the humans in the household, Donny and I have been together for about eight years.

What do the girls like? I would love to shop for them, but don't want to get things they wouldn't care about...Maybe you could give me a little inside info on them...Like do they like jewelry, games, something for their room?

How's the weather there? Last I heard from my mother it was already getting cold? It's cool at night here now but beautiful in the daytime (77-80).

Well guess I'd better go get ready for work. Thank you for the pictures of the girls! I love getting them!

Love,
Jana

Dana,

The chicks now have a corner in our shed until they get a little older and Donny will build a small shelter outside. We bring them in at night, as it is cooler now.

I do really like Palominos. Each neighbor is 4 acres apart, and we are surrounded by mountains. Sierra Vista is 20 miles away, with about any store you would need. Bisbee is also nearby, an old mining town with quaint little shops. There's so much history out here.

Yes, Lorna does still live in Florida and Dara and my brother Doug still live on Cape Cod near my mother.

That is correct, that my dad died shortly after your father and I divorced. I wanted to take you to see my mother and your father wouldn't let me. You and Amy were very close with my parents. They loved you so much. My father just glowed when the two of you were around...He died about 35 years ago when Dara was only 12 or 13.

My mother has any pics you have sent her on her refrigerator. She doesn't say a lot but I know she is very sad over us being separated. She had been so excited when you had gone to the reunion. I think she had many hopes for the future...

Yes, I'm sure after my mother recovers from surgery she would love to see you. That would really lift her spirits.

Love,
Jana

***

Following the cobblestone walkway to her front door on Cape Cod, I am about to knock when she pulls the door open and stands before me, small but steady on her feet. Her eyes show joy at my arrival, and I bend slightly to embrace her. After so many years of absence, I have found my way back to this grandmother who loves me.

She is always waiting for me to come back, my mother's mother. We are connected not only through blood, but through loss. In the *before* life, she was my doting grandmother, providing stability as my parents' marriage turned volatile.

So here I am again, finally. She shows me pictures of trips she took with her other grandchildren, weddings, new babies, all the things I never got to share with her. I teeter on the edge of bitterness for my loss. I mention my grandfather's death so many years ago, and instantly her eyes fill with tears. Today I see the past through her eyes, her daughter falling apart, her granddaughters slipping away, and then her husband dying, all while she is still raising teenagers. It is more than thirty-five years later and her grief is still raw.

When I am about to go, I tell her I will be back soon. I won't let more years go by; I promise. She holds on to my hand tightly and tries to speak but she can't. I know what she wants to say, a lifetime of words, but the void has swallowed them and all that is left in this moment is an understanding of love.

9
Healer

My mother's letters have been dwindling for the past several months, and when I offer to come visit, I don't get a response. When I try calling her, no matter the day, no one picks up. My brothers tell me that my mother's boyfriend is always yelling at our mother, and that their confrontations with him don't change anything, so they mostly stay away now. Kris tells me that he talks to our mother over the phone now and then, but when he invites her to his home, she declines. He is noticing her isolating more and more. I fear I will never reach her, never recover our bond.

"Why won't she let me in?" I ask the energy healer. I've come to see her because I feel I have nothing to lose. "During one phone call she said she'd be thrilled to have me visit, but then I don't hear from her for weeks. She keeps retreating when we start to get anywhere."

The woman closes her eyes, breathing deeply. Then she puts her hand over her heart, wincing, and says, "She can't." By all visible accounts, she is actually feeling my mother's pain. She opens her eyes and looks directly at me. Her eyes are the lightest, clearest blue I've ever seen. I look away for fear I may be hypnotized.

Now she has me laying on the table, and her hands hover above me, performing reiki. I can't control the shaking. My teeth are chattering. My whole body trembles. She tells me it is trauma leaving my body.

I am reminded of the time when I was twelve or thirteen and Dad initiated his one and only talk about our mother. He had been encouraged by a relative who was a psychiatrist to bring this topic up to Amy and me and so he was fulfilling his duty. He said only that the divorce had nothing to do with us kids and that our mother had loved us. I knew she did, I remembered. His words left me with so many questions, but I was afraid to ask any of them. Instead of speaking, I had started shaking and couldn't stop. "What's the matter, are you cold?" my father had asked. Amy didn't have questions either. At the end of the talk, he seemed satisfied, and took us out to lunch. I knew that had been my chance to speak, finally, and I hated myself for being such a coward.

"She can't," the healer says again. "She wants to, but it's as though she's been wearing a bandage to cover her gaping wound and now you want to rip it off. She can't handle it. She's been so hurt by so many people."

Why can't you help me get through to her? I want to ask. *Why are you making this sound so hopeless?* But I know she is just asserting the feeling she is getting, or *intuiting* as she'd prefer to call it.

She is saying what I've suspected but have been afraid to admit. I am finally ready to embrace my mother, to make up for at least *some* of our lost time, but now it might be too late.

My mother has gone to her happy place, the place of animals and their unconditional love, the place of dessert sun and mountains, a place where she never lost her children. My presence in her life threatens her sanity. I am a threat to her veil of denial.

I've wanted to shout at my mother, *It's me! Remember that little girl you left behind? The one who looks just like you? I survived and I haven't forgotten you! Don't you want me back?*

But I fear I am out of chances.

I would rather be told that my mother just doesn't care about me and never did. I would rather she be the bad mother my father wants me to believe she is. That is my best option. Not a wounded mother. Not a scared mother. A *bad* mother, an *abandoning* mother. Then I could say *I tried, but Dad was right.* But once you know the truth, you can't unknow it. My mother wasn't bad. She was deeply hurt, traumatized, perhaps beyond repair, and now I had become one of her offenders.

"You will write a memoir," the woman says with clarity.

She has just confirmed what I already know, or at least what I think to be true. I've wanted to write my story, to express through the written word what I have choked back all these years. She has tapped into my heart's desire and I tell her so.

"Why aren't you writing it all down already?" she asks.

"Because it isn't time yet?"

"Now is the perfect time. And don't worry, it will all come to you in chronological order. Once you commit to writing it down, the magic will happen. It will be powerful."

Chronological order. That's easy. I've got that already. Father abuses Mother. Mother has affairs. Father throws her out of home. I don't see her anymore. Many years later I am a mother. I must be a good mother. Yet I must know *her* to truly know *me*.

This is messed up. I must be messed up. I am *damaged goods*. I have always hated that expression because it is said in a way that implies permanent ruin, while I believe I am fixable. But now I am wondering if *I* have been the one to make the damage permanent.

For God's sake, be a good mother, was all I ever asked of myself. But I've pushed my children's grandmother away. I've ruined our chances at truly knowing her. I've let this loss go on for another generation. What have I done to stop the damage?

"You've been a good mother," this lady is saying now. "Say it," she instructs me. "Say, 'I've been a good mommy'."

Okay, I'll say it. "I've been a good mommy."

But I've made mistakes. I should do better.

If I was a better mother I wouldn't be here.

I wouldn't be *here*. Confused mothers come here. Desperate mothers. And I'm keeping it a secret. Good mothers don't keep secrets from their husbands. My husband would never do this. He's much too practical. And the waste of money. That is what would bother him the most, that I would spend good money on such a thing.

And yet I'm not sorry I'm here.

She can't tell me what to do to reach my mother though, or if there is any hope left at all. No one can tell me this. No one but God knows how the story ends, and now I wonder if God is shaking His head at me. *I gave you a chance, a good chance, you foolish, cowardly child, but you've squandered it!*

"Try to just let go of that, of wanting to know what will happen," she says now. She looks possessed, scared even, but just for the briefest of moments. Then she pulls herself quickly into the present and adds, "Just allow things to unfold."

I try to shake it off on the way home, tell myself that I was imagining her look of fear, that maybe she really didn't pause before telling me to "let things unfold."

I can't help but see her eyes though, remembering how they looked, icy and transfixed, pulled to some vision that I am left to imagine.

* * *

It has been a long time since I've heard from my mother, and now her home phone is disconnected and she no longer has a cell phone either. I have stayed in touch with my brother Kris, but being an almost four-hour drive from our mother, he cannot check on her with any regularity. Every couple of months I call her local police station and ask them to check on her, which they do. They report back that she says she is fine.

But I know that she is not fine. She has been abused by men since she was eighteen years old. She was bullied out of her children's lives and left with the shame that cloaks a mother without her children. She has one daughter who is unwilling to even respond to a heartfelt letter, and another daughter (me) who dangled reconnection in front of her heart and then yanked it away. Well into her sixties now, she works long hours and has high blood pressure, potentially untreated.

She is unreachable by phone or email and other than work and her overbearing boyfriend, she has been living in isolation.

I send her one more letter.

Dear Jana,

I was reading over some of your old letters to me – when you were still living on Cape Cod- and I felt very saddened and regretful about how poorly I handled our attempts to reconnect. I know I must have still been overly concerned with my father finding out about my being in touch with you. But I can no longer use that as an excuse as I am an adult with free will and simply needed to apply some critical thinking with some courage; it is so obvious to me now. I am so sorry. And I am sorry that you left Massachusetts (though I do understand the desire for warm weather, etc.). I wonder if I had handled things differently, if you might have stayed. And now to hear that you have no email and no phone makes me very worried that you are choosing to isolate.

You can always contact me if you want to, and I hope that you will. I have begun writing a memoir. I hope my writing the truth about what happened might bring you some peace of mind. If you have anything you want to write/add/say that you think will add clarity to the story, please do so. If not, that's okay too. I have a good understanding of what went on for you, thanks to our talks and letters over the years, however brief that time was.

I love you.
Dana

It's too late for us now, I know this. Even as I mail the letter, I expect silence.

I let her go.

PART THREE

Turning to face my past, shining a light down its dark hallways, finding where I left some part of myself. No one else is coming to get her.

10
Voice of the Alienated Child

In 2015, I tell my story at a Boston Moth live story-telling event and take first place. The theme on this particular night is *Adventure*. Each storyteller has five minutes to tell their story, so of course I don't tell my *whole* story. I tell of the night Amy and I showed up on our mother's doorsteps as teens, ten years after we had last seen her.

At the end of the event, several audience members congratulate me, and one young man adds, "I needed to hear that story." I wonder if he is alienated from a parent and if my story has urged him to consider reaching out to them. I can think of no better way to make meaning out of my own trauma than to help others with theirs.

Because I've won, I go on to tell my story again at the Moth's bigger venue. My husband and daughters are all there, supporting me. They are my reminder that no matter my story, I have a loving family right here, right now. I am nervous, but filled with gratitude.

I tell Amy about my Moth story after it is over. She seems quite happy that I've spoken on this topic, which takes me by surprise. She even sends me a congratulatory card. I think there is a part of her that longs to have her story told, too.

* * *

More and more, I am realizing that my story is not just *my* story. I begin speaking at alienated parent support groups, at fundraisers for the *Erasing Family Documentary*, and at the Massachusetts State House where the topic of shared custody is being discussed.

I've started an anonymous blog, a temporary container for my memoir (see Appendix A). I hear from hundreds of loving, hurting, alienated parents who are desperate for any tips I can share on how to recover their beloved children. I wish I had the answer for them, the key to gaining back their children, but all I can really offer is my own experience. I am a voice of the alienated child, and they know the pain of my mother. I get to know a few of these parents personally, and their stories break my heart open further. Many of them have fought in court, often over many years, to no avail. The ignorance, corruption, and breeding ground for antagonism that taints Family Court is remarkable. When one parent has stolen the mind of the child, and there are no negative consequences for that parent, the pathology thrives.

I keep writing, adding to my blog without sharing my name.

It feels purposeful and good and yet furtive at the same time. I hate how it is a secret from some, how I am hiding the fact that I am writing about my mother and the alienation. This particular type of abuse is insidious, epidemic, and yet I hide out in the shadows, a phantom writer, hoping to somehow contribute to the solution.

11
Last Chance

I have been unable or unwilling to write lately, paralyzed by something, stalled and uncertain. What has it been? Fear? Restlessness? I have this feeling that I should move forward somehow, take some action, try something again. I contact my brother lamenting about not being able to reach our mother, and how I had let go, but it just didn't feel right anymore. What else could I do?

His response gives me hope. Our mother has a phone again, and he gives me the number. Could I call her? After her silence, our lack of any communication these last several years, could I just pick up the phone and call her?

It takes me two weeks to finally make the call, but when I do, she answers.

We talk, small talk at first but it quickly turns to the past. I am surprised by her willingness to go there, but we do. Through tears she tells me again that she regrets not fighting for me all those years ago. I give her my complete forgiveness, my complete understanding. And I apologize for not standing up to my father too, in adulthood, and instead, pushing her away. We talk and cry.

She tells me she is planning to visit her mother soon, this summer. My grandmother is ill and won't live much longer. My mother is eager to go to her, on Cape Cod. I tell her I want to meet her at her mother's house and she sounds happy about this. Perhaps her mother's impending death has given her the courage to open her heart to me again. I hold on to this chance like it is a fragile lifeline, a frayed thread of connection. I am grasping it gently, carefully.

If I let go of it, our lives will pass by without seeing each other again. This I am sure of.

* * *

On the Wednesday before Labor Day weekend, my mother calls me from Cape Cod. I ask about my grandmother and about my mother's flight from Arizona. I offer to drive to my grandmother's house the very next day, where my mother is staying. She agrees, and then we hang up.

The next morning, I go through my closet. What does one wear when they haven't seen their mother in twenty years? *She is still my mother.* No matter what has happened, truth feels good.

It is a beautiful, sunny drive to my grandmother's house, and I am eager to take the scenic left turn down her street, just past a crimson stretch of cranberry bog. My grandparents used to take us to Cape Cod frequently in the summertime in my *before* life, but I've only been here sporadically since then. It is strange to wonder how many things would be different if I had stayed close to my maternal family.

When my mother answers the door, I think how lovely she still is at seventy years old. She says hello, cheerfully, smiling. I reach out and we hug.

Inside my grandmother's split-level home, my mother leads me up the stairs and into the living room. My grandmother smiles brightly while saying my name. I am told she's been going in and out of consciousness and sometimes forgetting who people are. But today she is alert, even walking about a bit, albeit slowly.

I see my Aunt Dara too, who has been taking care of her mother alone before Jana arrived. I am happy to be with all of them, these women I have loved, still love. And although I am on the outside, the one left behind, we are all connected.

My mother and I go for a walk. We talk of the weather and of my grandmother's end of life. We talk of my daughters, all grown up now, and of family resemblances. We speak about the ocean and of her quiet life in Arizona. I mention Amy and her eyes fill with tears.

I can feel her regret that is so vast it could swallow her; I think her grief might turn her to particles, to the dust in the desert she lives in.

I want to say, "I wish you would move back to Massachusetts. I want to spend time with you, to make up for lost years. I want you to know my husband and our daughters."

I want my mother back. I don't want her to live two thousand and five hundred and seventy-two miles away for one more day. But I don't say any of this. Instead, I ask, "Don't you miss the ocean?"

When it is time for me to go, we hug goodbye and both say how happy we are to have had this day. We agree that we want to stay in touch, but we make no promises, no unrealistic mention of all the time we will spend together, knowing she will fly back to Arizona, to her life there.

* * *

We talk on the phone sometimes now. We are getting to know each other again.

I need her to know something. I say, "I know you had planned to keep Amy and me with you when we were kids. I know that was your plan."

There is a long pause and I wait while she cries, quietly. She is relieved that I know this.

"I love you," I hear her say. "I always have."

I say I love her too. And then I ask about her day.

12
Truth

Shortly after my grandmother's passing, I am on the phone with my Uncle Doug, my mother's brother. I share my childhood memory of him holding my father against the wall by the t-shirt.

He knows right away what I am talking about. He tells me that he had just witnessed my father hitting my mother that day. My father thought my uncle had left our house, but he had only gone into the bathroom, next to the back door. He came out after hearing a scuffle, and saw my mother holding her face in pain, flushed and tear-streaked. "I'd just gotten back from Vietnam," my uncle said. "And I was trained to kill. When I saw your father hit my sister, it set me off. I remember it was evening and you and Amy were in your little footie pajamas. I grabbed your father by the shirt and then by the throat and had him pinned to the wall. He couldn't breathe until I let him go and he slid down the wall."

This memory had been seared in my mind; the white t-shirt gathered in my uncle's fist, the kitchen wall, my father's red face.

"I told Jana to gather you girls and leave with me right then, but she refused. I couldn't believe it. I stopped speaking to her for a long time after that night. And we had been close."

I tell him how hard I think it was for her to leave, and how scary. I want to explain what I've learned about trauma bonds and battered women syndrome, but I don't.

"I really believe she was a loving mother," I say.

"Oh my God, yes," he says, tearing up now. "She loved you and your sister so much. She was so proud of you girls. She was the most loving mother, there's no denying that." This is validating and heart wrenching at the same time.

Several people who knew my mother and me back then say the same thing. *She was a loving mother. She adored her children. She was kind.*

My father worked two jobs, belonged to a country club, had friends outside the marriage. My mother was very often alone with us kids; alone and feeling trapped in a marriage that was making her miserable. Was she wise to seek comfort from other men? Was she executing a good escape by planning to run away with one of them? Hell, no.

But also, how much loyalty does a woman owe her abuser? And did cheating on my father make her unworthy of being my mother? Was it grounds for desecrating her bond with her children? My mother may have made some bad choices, but ditching her children was never her plan.

Despite the evidence I have of our mother's love, Amy and I see things from different lenses, different realities. She sums the past up as, "our parents both made mistakes." I believe she joined an alliance with my father when she was five, one that she was coerced into, and although I am certainly guilty of going along, the only way to truly fully join them in their reality would be to give up my own.

Mothers always got custody back then, is a line I heard as evidence that our mother *must* be awful, since she did not get custody of us. The implication changes back and forth from *She walked out on us* to *She lost custody because she is dangerous.* During a phone call I had with my stepmother once, in a rare mention of the past, she said, "Your father's lawyer had told us not to let you go outside alone. *She* might try to take you." So, which was it? She didn't want us or she was going to come steal us back? It is disturbing how easily a persecutory delusion can spread.

One day I was calmly asserting to Amy the cruelty of our father erasing our entire maternal family, and how devastating that was for all of them. In a rare moment of belief, she said, "I hope Dad never realizes what he did, that he took so many people down. Imagine how he might feel if he faced that."

* * *

I tell Amy that our grandmother has passed.

Thanks for letting me know, she says.

As always, I hold out hope that she will remember, in a flash, the love.

But instead, I feel the distance grow wider between us. The more I dare to mention *that family*, the greater the divide. Still, I send her a copy of our grandmother's obituary. It mentions our grandmother's nursing career, her service to her community, the way she always cared for others. It also includes words about her family and how much she loved her grandchildren, all fourteen of us. I include a note to Amy:

We were two of the thirteen grandchildren. We were the firsts.

* * *

There is one question I wish I had asked my Uncle Doug but didn't. Did he tell my grandparents about the abuse he had witnessed? And if so, did they try to help my mother?

But if I am being honest with myself, I already know the answer. On one of my phone calls with my mother, one in which I wanted to hear more of her story, she told me that my father once dropped her off at her parents' home with a black eye. "Do something about your daughter," he had said at the door, and then left. I did not ask my mother if this was following her first infidelity, but I assumed it was. *Even for someone as audacious as my father,* and *even back in the late 1960s when domestic violence was still fairly common,* and *even when the male in question had charmed his wife's parents into accepting him, he still would have needed to justify why his wife "deserved it."*

The bigger point though, much bigger than *what my mother had done* in order for my father to feel so free to expose his form of punishment to her parents, was that *they knew*. Even if my grandparents somehow remained clueless of the emotional and verbal abuse — the yelling, intimidating, controlling — they got a front row seat that day to the physical abuse.

Whether or not my Uncle Doug told them about what *he* witnessed at my home, my grandparents knew that my mother was physically abused. If there is a place where facts can go that is halfway between denial and conscious thought, that is where this has lived in me. I haven't wanted to believe this about my beloved grandparents, but I cannot forget what my mother told me. I knew she was telling me the truth, and I quieted the part of me that wanted to know more. *Why didn't they try to help you move out? Did they discourage you from returning to him or did they encourage it because you'd "made your bed?"*

And if they encouraged her to go home and work things out, do they get a pass because this was the 1960s and they believed it was more important to keep a family together than to escape abuse? If they get a pass, does my father get a pass for simply being the husband he was taught to be? When you know better you do better and no one involved knew better, right?

But there was something *even* darker in store than your typical domestic violence, and I think my mother sensed it back then, before the divorce. Even if my grandparents had made it an option for my mother to stay with them, my father would not have let her take us with her. She had told me emphatically, "There was no discussing custody with your father." It was win or lose, and he wasn't going to lose. And if my mother had a chance at a civil divorce, without fear and abuse, I don't believe for one minute she would have kept us from seeing our father.

13
Silent Goodbye

It is just five years after my grandmother's death when my brother reaches out to tell me that my mother has had a stroke and is in a hospital in Arizona. He visits her and keeps me updated, but all of it sounds terribly depressing. She hadn't been taking her medicine as prescribed. She would need rehabilitation to walk and talk coherently again. Her boyfriend is insisting she skip rehab and come straight home with him. My brother does his best to insist she do what the doctor is advising. She does in fact go to rehab, but only for a short time before she is home again, fending for herself.

Not long afterwards, a second stroke lands her back in the hospital, and this time she isn't going anywhere. Her heart is giving out.

Her boyfriend answers when I call the hospital, and he rants and raves and cries to me that he doesn't know how he will live without "his baby." I am thinking, *well you should've thought of that sooner and been nice to her, asshole.* But then I remember I have been no prize either, and I don't want him to hang up on me, so I refrain from sharing my thoughts with him. He puts the phone to her ear, and I tell her she is a good mother. I tell her I love her.

He tells me she is smiling.

* * *

I have an old newspaper clipping hung up over my desk; it's a photograph of my mother when she was about eight or nine years old. She is at Santa's Village in New Hampshire with her family and she's feeding a baby goat with a bottle. Santa's Village is open year-round, and it looks like it is spring, or maybe very early summer in the picture. She is wearing a powder- blue sweater and has her hair tied back with a ribbon. The caption says, *Jana Corbin, of Hudson, Mass., feeds a baby goat with a bottle of milk bought at Santa's Workshop.*

I often take the clipping down to study it. She is smiling, and if I look closely, I see that her eyes are aimed right at the baby goat's mouth, watching it take the milk. She looks so focused, and so content, I wonder if she even realized someone was photographing her. She is so innocent, so precious.

The girl in the photograph is so completely unaware of how her life is going to turn out. She will nurture more animals, and babies, and her heart will get shattered. But even though it makes me sad to look at it, it makes me smile, too. I know in that moment in time, before life ravaged her, she was free.

* * *

My sister and I are sitting outside having coffee at a café when I get a text from my Aunt Dara that our mother has passed. I had been telling Amy that it was just a matter of time, and she had asked if I thought she should call our mother. "What would you say?" I had asked, and before she could answer, I added, "No, I don't think you should."

So, it is both unsurprising and jolting at the same time, to be sitting here with Amy when the news comes. I read Dara's text aloud: *I'm so sorry, honey. Jana has passed away. Call me if you want to talk. I am here for you.* Amy watches me, waiting for my reaction, but I simply look her in the eye silently. I send my mother a silent goodbye, the last one.

"I feel so strange right now," Amy says.

"I'm going to tell Dad she died," I declare. "I am going to tell him because you are supposed to tell your father when your mother dies and I am going to do the *normal* thing."

"Good! I think you should," she answers.

"It wasn't normal or right to feel like I couldn't even mention her to him," I add. "I have been in touch with my brother, my aunt, and my grandmother too, it isn't right that it feels like a secret." I say this with conviction and my sister is nodding, agreeing, and she seems like she means it. She seems like she *wants* me to tell our father the news. She asks if I want her to be there, and I say no. I know that if I bring up the topic of our mother to our father, that this time I am leaving no words unspoken.

14
Choices

It is about three weeks before Thanksgiving, and Carl and I are planning to host our annual turkey dinner at our home, to include our daughters and their families or significant others, my sister Amy and her family, my father and stepmother, and an aunt and uncle.

I have a lot to be thankful for. Our daughters and granddaughters are thriving, and Carl and I feel close to all of them. We are healthy, as in love as ever, and I've published my first book to boot, which is the culmination of many essays I had written as our children were growing. In it, I even included a chapter called *Healing* in which I touch upon my mother loss. I am taking care of myself and feel like I have long since processed my old trauma and am living consciously, purposefully.

But despite my ongoing healthy habits, my yoga practice and meditation, my writing and speaking to audiences about alienation, I have yet to gather the courage or the will to bring up my mother's death to my father. My husband has supported me facing my father on this topic, has listened and understood as I've told him over and over that I *just need to say it.* Not only do I need to say that she died, but that I know she wasn't a bad mother. I know now that I was responsible for pushing her away in my earlier adult years, and this is a painful truth, a deep regret that I have to live with. But while I work on my own regrets, I also need to speak the truth to my father. I have been feeling so out of integrity with speaking and writing about my experience while at the same time pretending, by omission of my truth, to go along with the family narrative that my father created five decades ago now. I need to hold myself to a standard of honesty, instead of controlling his reaction by *not* speaking up. I need to prove to myself that I am no longer silenced, that I can choose to speak.

Several months have gone by now since our mother's death, and Amy is strongly encouraging me to talk to my father like I said I was going to. I know I should, but I am filled with dread whenever I imagine doing so. The last time I brought up my mother to him, twenty-five years ago now, it went terribly. He asked me to never bring it up again. But that was then, and I was a lot more vulnerable to his declarations of innocence, his pleas for pity, his anger at the mention of her name. When I bring it up this time, there will be no backing down for me. I know that bringing up my mother's death will just be the opening line and then I will spill the truth of what I know, words that will land like acetone on the picture he painted for the world to see long ago.

* * *

Anyone who has done even a lick of trauma research knows that there are four main responses: *Fight, flight, freeze* and *fawn*. Usually, we have one or two that we favor, and my top reflexes in times of stress have been *freeze* and *fawn*.

I feel that the *fight* response would have served me better in my life. I would've stood a chance of an earlier, lasting reconnection with my mother. I would have *fought* for my right to have a relationship with her rather than freezing or fawning to avoid conflict with those who expected my unquestioning loyalty. Or in the case of *flight*, I would've left my family of origin at the age of eighteen or twenty-one, or after my father's response to my email back when I was in my thirties. I would have *fled* the people who insisted on my silence. A line in the sand would have forced a different outcome; stop denying my truth or I go. Once gone, I would've been able to have a relationship with my mother without worrying about consequences for disrupting the status quo. I would not have just seen through the haze of gaslight; I would have *left* it.

But instead, my freeze and fawn responses kept me from acting in my own best interest, from speaking up and telling my truth. Finding the letters from my mother and grandmother that were hidden from me, the visit to my maternal family as a teen, the one-and-done talk Dad had with us to explain our "mother situation," the adoption, the "Are we good?" moment with Dad after I'd sent him the email; during these moments and so many others, I froze or fawned. Becoming mute, placating, staying stuck in a situation that does not serve me at all, avoiding conflict; I abandoned myself every damn time.

It has taken me a long time to finally suppress my habitual responses when I am under stress. It seems the more intense the distress I feel, the more my outdated responses are triggered. But I *can* find my voice and my legs — to shout, to act, to leave — even when I am fearful. Granted, instead of feeling instinctual, it feels like I am forcing myself through quicksand. I've had to learn that acting from a place of self-love is not comfortable. It often means doing the opposite of what my primal brain wants me to do.

Part of living consciously is becoming aware of our tendencies and then choosing differently. My childhood trauma may have elicited my freeze and fawn responses, and perhaps those were necessary at the time, but once I became an adult, it was *my* responsibility to change what needed changing. I wish I had grasped this concept earlier in life. I've become a firm believer in tending to our own wounds, and although I can attribute some faulty coping mechanisms to my past, I can no longer use the past as an excuse to hold on to them. Afterall, if I let myself off the hook, then I've got to let everyone off the hook. Everyone who hurts anyone, including themselves, is just reacting from their childhood pain. If I render myself helpless to old patterns, then I must render everyone else helpless too; victims of old trauma forevermore.

As Amy is encouraging me to reach out to our father, and tell him about our mother's death, I keep trying to imagine how it will go.

Nothing in my mind's eye looks easy or comfortable, not by a long shot. But I have to give this an honest effort at communicating what I have held back all my life. *Holding back my truth* is not serving anyone. I have to do this with courage and confidence, not just for myself, but for my mother. I have to set the record straight, even if it is in her death.

* * *

"Dana, Mom is going to be out of the house from about one o'clock to three o'clock today. I am picking her up to come dress shopping with me. Dad will be alone. You could call him then." Amy has orchestrated my opportunity and I know I shouldn't procrastinate any longer.

I tell Carl I am going to do it. He had always encouraged me to speak more openly to my father about the past, thinking that it would be a chance for us to form a better father-daughter relationship. Years ago, when he helped me compose the email to my father, he thought that my father, faced with his daughter's heartfelt desire to talk, might actually hear me. *How could a father not listen? How could he not want to do his best to repair this? How could he not have empathy for his own child?* At the time, I found his optimism both enviable and flawed. Today, his expectations for my father are different, more realistic. Even still, he knows I feel the need to open this conversation again, no matter the response I am likely to get.

As one o'clock approaches, I pace, I rehearse the first words, the only ones I have planned out. *My mother died.*

Now it is one-thirty.

Now one-forty-five. I put my cell phone on the coffee table and stare at it. I pick it up. I put it down.

Two o'clock.

I pick up my phone and I call. Now I stand up and walk just the perimeter of the living room while my father's phone rings. He answers and we chitchat briefly. Then I push my emotions down, I cut them off. I tell my father that I am calling to tell him something. I speak from my head only. I am intentionally making this call from the neck up so my emotions don't overwhelm me

"I am not sure *why* I am telling you Dad, but my mother died," I say clearly, almost matter-of-factly.

"Well, it is always sad when someone dies," he says. He doesn't sound surprised. In fact, from the moment he picked up the phone he sounded expectant and uneasy. I suspect Amy has warned him this was coming.

Our call can't end here. I didn't just call him to tell him my mother died. He doesn't give two shits about my mother. He would've been glad if she died long ago. No, that's not why I am really calling.

"She had a terrible adult life, Dad," I say, knowing exactly where this is about to go. There is a pause.

"Well, she made her choices."

And that sentence was all the permission, all the opening I needed to let the words come.

"She made her choices? Which choices, Dad? It wasn't the simple story of 'she just left' that you wanted us to believe."

"What do you mean it wasn't that simple?" he says now and his voice has changed. He is defensive now, angry. I feel my own anger start to rise up, but I don't let it overtake me. I stay in my head.

I am pacing. Carl had stepped outside because he thought I might want privacy, but now I wave him back in. He witnesses my end of the call.

I tell my father what I mean. I tell him what I know. I say that my mother was afraid of him, and that I was too. I tell him it makes no sense that she would simply abandon her children. She was a good mother. She loved us. She was not a monster who discards her children because she's bored of them. She wasn't a drug addict or abuser or anything of the sort.

I tell him I know he wanted to punish her. That she couldn't be his wife and therefore he wouldn't let her be our mother.

He is silent now. I think I have surprised him with this last line. He didn't expect anyone to get inside his head that way. But in addition to my own instincts, and the conversations I've had with my mother and others, I've done my research. I've done my homework, years of it, and his mind works like every alienator's mind.

"You can't put me in a box," he says. "You don't know what I was thinking. It was very complicated."

"You're not taking responsibility for any of it," I say now. Carl gives me a thumbs up. I feel it is going terribly because nothing has changed with him since I attempted this conversation the last time, twenty-something years ago.

But Carl's endorsement is because of how I am handling it this time. *I* have changed.

"It was complicated," he repeats. "I was young." He stops.

"I know you were young, Dad. And you had been abused by your father. And he abused your mother." I was trying to give him his excuses so he could admit some fault. I was trying to let him know that I understood why he might have done what he did, given his background.

"I am nothing like my father." He is adamant. "In fact, I am probably the *opposite* of my father."

Opposite? I want to laugh sarcastically, but it feels too mean. I don't feel vengeful. I just need my silence to end.

"You're not taking any responsibility, Dad," I say.

"You're not giving me a chance to," he answers.

I take deep breath.

Is he contemplating going down another path? Is he going to admit fault? It is all it would take for me to forgive. I want to forgive.

Silence.

I speak again. "Why did we never see our grandparents again, Dad? Even if Jana was the abandoning monster you want to pretend she was, why were her parents shut out of our lives? They loved us."

"I……They didn't ask to see you." His voice says he knows how ridiculous this excuse is even as he says it.

"If you need to cut me out of your life, I'll be heartbroken, but…," he starts to say.

It seems he is telling me he'd rather never speak to me again than have this conversation. He has already jumped to cutting ties. I don't respond to that. I am not done trying.

"So let me get this straight, Dad. My mother and my grandparents never wanted to see me again. Is that what you are saying? I want to be clear. They never wanted to see me again? That was what they chose? Is this what you are claiming?"

I have found my voice and I am not afraid. I am holding my father accountable for the first time in my life, for robbing me of my mother, my maternal family. I am naming his abuse and I am not backing down.

I mention the day my mother visited me on my birthday and how I couldn't tell her I wanted her to stay. I had to appease *him*. I say I know he remarried within a year or so, and we were already calling his new wife "Mom" when our real mother visited. I talk about Amy being coaxed to reject our mother.

"You are just making up stories because you want to have a memoir."

I am a bit stunned, but I don't respond to this. I am still.

"If you want to believe your mother loved you, go ahead but…"

I silently take it in. I take in my father's decision to not admit any fault, to not show any empathy, not then, not now, not ever.

"Meg just got home. We are going to have to continue this conversation another time," he says

He is in a hurry to hang up now.

There is nothing left to say anyway.

"Bye." I hang up.

"I am so proud of you," Carl says. "I would not have believed it if I hadn't heard it. I would not have believed you stood up to your father like you did."

But my worst predictions are true. My truth is so distasteful to my father that he'd rather cut ties than admit that anything I am saying is accurate. He will sacrifice me in order to keep his lies intact. I feel I've proven what I've known all along; to him, I am only as good as my willingness to stay silent.

The response was not really different from twenty-five years ago. Sure, I stood up to my father this time. But in the end, the choice is the same: shut up or ship out. My old therapist, Dr. Johnson, was right. I was afraid to express myself as a child because I felt I'd be outcasted, like my mother. Like I am about to be now.

15
Shunned

I brace myself for Amy's phone call, which comes the next day. She thought I was simply going to tell Dad that our mother had died. *What happened? She is shocked. She thought it was going to go well. In fact, she had given him and our stepmother a heads up. She'd gone to their home and discussed the situation with them ahead of time, so they'd be prepared. She'd told them that I was in touch with an aunt, a brother, and that I didn't want to keep it a secret. They were good about it! All I had to do was tell them about Jana's death and it would've been so fine. What had I done?*

From her perspective, I changed the script. I was just supposed to tell him that our mother died. But I never said I wasn't going to bring up the past. I never made any promises at all, so I don't feel I owe her an explanation, but because old patterns die hard, I give her one anyway. *I hadn't planned out all that I would say to our father, but yes, I brought up the past to him and I'd been meaning to for quite some time,* I tell her.

Our conversation gets heated and then we hang up. A couple weeks go by and I accept that my father is not going to call me back to finish our conversation, and perhaps that is for the best. Word gets back to me through Amy that our sister Julie and our stepmother are very upset with me as well. In their minds, I am the offender, the villain, while poor old Dad, on the verge of cognitive decline, is the victim.

Why would I bring this up after all these years?

Why would I upset Dad this way when he was aging, had done his best?

How could I do this? How could I knowingly blow up the family?

Their reactions would seem reasonable to me if I was bringing up something much smaller, like, say Dad had given the family pet away when I was a child and I just can't let it go. Then perhaps I'd be out of line, digging up an old wound, one that I should've dealt with on my own. But for the love of God, I am talking about my *mother*. I want to let go of this, I really do. But it is even harder to forget what was done to my mother than to forgive what was done to me. It ruined her life. She never recovered, and now she is dead.

I text my stepmother to tell her we are cancelling the get together. *Since Dad accused me of making up stories, I don't see any clear path to reconciling. I think it is best for everyone if we do not get together for Thanksgiving.* I chose my father's most offensive line to give as the reason why I could not see them. Accusing me of being a liar, of making things up, in order to write a book was about as low as he could have gone. It was the sentence that made it so very clear that if I dared to speak the truth, and if I didn't accept his defense, he would simply call me a liar.

My stepmother bluntly agrees there is no path forward and that cancelling is best. And for a few moments, I feel relieved, free. *I won't have to stay and engage in the impossibility of defending myself because they aren't having me anyway.*

I've been wanting to speak my mind, my truth, since I was a little child, and I just couldn't bring myself to do it. I'd tried several years ago, and failed. There had never been, and never would be, a *good* time, an *acceptable* time to talk to my father about the past; not when I was four or fourteen or thirty-four and clearly not now.

But now, finally, I had. And the consequence of that is as bad as I thought it would be; the reactions of others is as tough as I'd imagined. But I've done it.

For weeks I am reeling from my outcast position, from the familial punishment that has resulted from speaking my truth. Although the backlash is not at all surprising, it temporarily ignites an anger in me that I welcome. I welcome the anger because it keeps me from slipping into the old temptation to placate others in order to calm my nervous system. It keeps me from obsessing over if I was too firm, too direct, should I have been gentler with my father? I had thought that speaking my truth would feel better, would set me free, and I am still hopeful that it will. For now, though, I am a prisoner of my discomfort. I'm fumbling for the key, trying to release myself from doubt and anxiety. When the anger comes, it reminds me that it is okay if I didn't do it perfectly.

I sign up for twelve online therapy sessions and I make it a goal to process my feelings within that time. I also want guidance in navigating the future of these relationships. I describe the guilt that threatens to overcome me, and my therapist tells me that I haven't done anything wrong. She tells me to stay in *my own* experience and out of my father's experience of this. I need to hear it over and over. My husband tells me I am the most loving person he knows, and I want to wear his words like a shield. Intellectually, I know I have a right to speak my reality, but my skin is not yet thick enough to absorb being treated like the villain. I hate that I still need others' reassurance.

Nearly a month goes by with no contact from my father. I tell my new therapist that I am struggling with whether or not cutting all ties would actually be the best for us. Some days it feels like it's already happened, and that we both want this. Other days, that solution seems too extreme. The therapist listens and commends me for my thoughtfulness. She reminds me there is no right or wrong answer here, just a very painful situation that I am doing my best to navigate. But I want there to be a right answer, and I want her to tell me what it is.

There is a family wedding coming up that we are expected to be at, *want to* be at. And my father and stepmother will be there too. How can this work? This is one of many such situations that are likely to occur. There are aunts and uncles, nieces and nephews, other generations. Is avoiding each other really a viable solution? The best solution?

* * *

I decide to reach out and invite my father to meet for coffee and he accepts. My husband is concerned, but I've reasoned that it will make things easier for us, our children, everyone, if my father and I can be on speaking terms. My logic is convincing. Cordiality. Peace. I've said what I needed to say and I need to minimize the drama in my life. Cutting all ties would be dramatic. Even as I say this, I don't really know what the right answer is. Then I remember to take the pressure off myself to *know* what is best. There is no playbook for this.

Am I imagining that my father looks disheveled when he exits his car? He greets me with a hug as if no harsh words were ever said between us. His tone is kind. Minus my torturing him with this *mother topic*, he has been proud of me. He knows I live a good life, and I married a good man. He doesn't have to worry about me; he has said as much. He is proud of my children too. In his own way, he loves me, loves all of us.

When we sit down inside, I want to forget everything and just have pleasant small talk, a girl and her father. He is getting old and given the state of our relationship, I don't know how many more times I will see him. But I get right to the point. I tell him that I brought up the past because I needed to be honest with him about it. I say I know that we are never going to find common ground on this topic, and that I am willing to drop it for the sake of peace.

"I just was absolutely devastated, blind sighted, when you brought this up after fifty years," he says.

In his mind, he is the victim. He will never show remorse, not toward me and certainly not toward my deceased mother. To him, to my whole family of origin, I am the problem. I know this, and I accept it. I accept it as I feel my self-created shield, a boundary as big as the Grand Canyon, separating my whole self from the rest of this family.

"I had to stand up for myself and my mother, Dad," I say firmly. "I had to speak up for both of us." He doesn't refute this. He looks at me like he knows he shouldn't challenge this now. I could even interpret it as a look of surrender. In this moment, and perhaps forevermore, I think that is the best he is able to do; to say nothing. And I leave it at that.

I'm not sure anymore that it was my father's lack of any remorse that kept me from forgiving him all these years. I had been complacent, stuck in a web of silence that made forgiveness impossible. In speaking out I did not receive his validation, or an apology, or even a desire to actually hear me. But I earned self-respect because I told the truth. I walked into the lion's den because I'd left something behind, and now I never have to go back. That something was my voice. Even though my father may think of my speaking out as his worst nightmare, it is the very thing that has allowed me to set him free.

16
My Own Good Mother

When I ponder over the many blessings of my life, marriage and motherhood have been among the greatest. There's a theory that we should give away what we most want, and I think that is what I did in motherhood. I gave away the love and nurturing that eluded me as a child, and I did so happily. In doing so, I benefitted too. The chance to be a mother, a loving mother, has always felt like a calling and a gift.

Loving and being loved so well by my husband has been healing too. Some might say that I married too soon, that I should have been tending to my past and my healing before settling down; and they would have a valid point, one that I have contemplated myself. But I keep coming back to how very right marriage and motherhood have felt to me. I believe it was Grace that brought my husband into my life at such a young age. Could it be that we need to experience love in order to heal? If we require ourselves to fully heal *before* giving or receiving love, we may be waiting forever.

No one has forever. I feel this deeply on my drive home from yoga class recently. Like an epiphany, I suddenly feel the significance of *every single choice*. Days morph into years, but choices, one by one, morph into a life. And every choice, including the small ones, bring us closer or further from our true selves. Time did not wait for me while I pondered reaching out to my mother or writing my memoir or speaking to my father. Every single moment is a chance to make another choice. I don't ever want to squander this again.

I had a dream that I found my child-self. She was sitting in a corner, arms wrapped around her knees. When I saw her, I was so happy and filled with so much love. I felt a love that I have always felt for my children, but never for myself. I told her how very happy I was to see her. "I will take care of you," I said in my dream, decidedly. I will be my own good mother.

She is the child that holds my memories. She knows my grief, but I've made it less important now that she reveal every detail. *Not knowing* if I cried out for my mother, or if I sought comfort, or when my tears stopped, no longer plagues me. The more important thing now is that I have come back for her, and taken her by the hand. I am leading her forward.

APPENDIX A
An Alienated Daughter's Blog
The Virus

The disgrace fallen upon the out-cast parent can be shockingly insidious. Like a virus, it is invisible, cunning, and harmful.

It is not just adults who catch the virus. I can recall sitting outside with my sister and a neighborhood friend about a year or two after my mother was cast out of my life. We were young children, and one of us brought up the subject of my mother, a very rare occurrence. Our neighbor, a little girl of about six years old, said, incredulously, "*I remember she used to give us whole bottles of coke!*" She was referring to the individual bottles of Coca-Cola. It wasn't what she said that spoke volumes, but the tone in which she said it, implying that our mother was *a bad, irresponsible mother.* This was a friend who had been welcomed into our home by our mother, and treated kindly. Somehow, even this innocent little girl had gotten on board the hate wagon.

This influence spread far and wide and each time I was witness to it, I remained silent. I only had four years with my mother; how could I prove to anyone that she was good? I was a child when she disappeared from my life, and I was expected to believe she simply didn't want me. How does a young child explain that her heart tells her otherwise, while living in an atmosphere that forbids such declaration?

An Alienated Daughter's Blog

Solving the Mystery

A few years after the mysterious disappearance of my mother, my sister and I found a kite in our yard that did not belong to us. We took it upon ourselves to travel about the neighborhood, searching for its rightful owner. It was a challenge, a game of sorts, to try to find the child who had lost his kite.

But to me, it felt like more than a game. It wasn't that I was overly concerned with the kite owner's loss; it was that I had an unfulfilled need to *solve a mystery*. It felt urgent to me, like an obsession, or an all-consuming task. The mystery had landed in my own backyard, and I had a burning desire to get to the bottom of it.

Maybe if I could solve the tiny mysteries, someday I would find out the big truths.

To my disappointment, we never did find out who the kite belonged to, but I never forgot that day, or the feeling that was evoked in me. I recognized that feeling again at eighteen, when I searched my parents' divorce files at the courthouse, looking for clues. And again, as an adult when I contacted my mother's lover, the one who was going to help her escape her marriage.

My truth seeking finally led me to my mother, where I could get her story. It also led me to other family members who could help me to fill in some missing pieces, or in many cases, validate what my childhood memories held.

She was a loving mother.

It is not easy being a truth seeker when much of the truth is ugly. But here's the thing: the truth is beautiful too. I have not sought evidence against my father, as much as I have sought evidence *for my mother*.

And although it has taken me decades, the clues were easy to find. They have been tucked away in my heart and memories my whole life. The years, and the seeking, were just an excavation of what was there. I already knew.

An Alienated Daughter's Blog

To My Father and to Every Alienator

I know that no one is born revengeful or angry. I believe that people enter life as love. I know that you were abused by your father, who was likely abused by his and so on. I know that his words probably did more damage than his fist- the way he told you that you were worthless, incapable, nothing. He didn't see you, not really. He told you a lie.

I know that he abused your mother, my grandmother. She told me about the time when you were a teen and had enough of his wrath. The time, the hundredth time, he banged his fist and stood up at the dinner table; something trivial triggered his rage and when he leaned toward your mother, you stood to protect her. You ran to grab the ax used for cutting wood and told him no more. He sat back down. You drew a line that day.

But you drew a line over your heart too. The line says *I will love this much but no more. I will feel this much but no more.*

It reasons, this line you've drawn, that you did your best to love *my* mother and she rejected you. Your best was sometimes cold, mean, and demeaning, but perhaps it was better than what you knew. The line says you *will not feel sadness. You will not grieve.*

The line says you will feel *this* but not *that. Anger* but not *grief. Rage* but not *compassion.* I was not allowed to grieve either, when you cast my mother out. Your actions were cut off from your heart, your spirit. Even your supposed love for me could not lift you above this rage, this protection you had built for yourself. You had to win. Win at hurting. Win at all costs.

I was expected to put the same line over my heart, a line that says *I will not love my mother. I will let her go.* And the cost was great, much greater than your ego knows. Your ego thinks you won; it even thinks I won, for I have you, the superior one.

But your spirit knows you have lost. The choices you made were from wounds and from fear, and not from love, not from love at all, despite what you may have convinced yourself.

Love does not do this.

You may never own this, not before your death anyway. You sense that if you did, you would feel a pain much greater than your father's fist. Greater than his cutting words. Greater than the pain of rejection. You would feel a pain as searing as an ax through the heart. To face what you have done would mean facing all your wounds. It would render you vulnerable. But in letting it break your heart, you would find your true self. If you only knew what you stand to gain.

For now, my father, and Every Alienator, you are existing in a swath of protection, in a lie that tells you that you have won, that you are right. But that lie is fragile, weak and thin, and it covers your heart where the truth resides. That is what you don't know; you don't know the cost of *winning.*

I take comfort in knowing the truth. I have suffered great blows to my sense of self, but I am thankful that I am a truth seeker.

If you allow yourself to break apart, to see the truth, I will not say *I told you so.*

Someday, maybe not in this lifetime, I will see the real you and I will recognize you as love.

An Alienated Daughter's Blog

All That You Never Asked: A Message to My Stepmother

You were young and unsuspecting, and eager to leave your mother's home.

My father wrote you love poems and promised to make you queen of his castle.

He needed to replace my mother you see, and you never asked why.

You cut my hair short to match your own and we never mentioned Her.

It was convenient after all, to have your husband's ex-wife cast aside and out of our lives.

She had left home, gone away, my father told you. You never asked why.

Then one day she showed up, eyes full of grief. Shaking in my father's presence, she handed me a birthday gift. I had just turned five.

Jealous and crying, you looked to my father to console you while I opened the gift.

I was scared to ask my mother to stay. Terrified to say how much I've missed her.

From my room at night, I heard you and my father fighting, loud and violent.

I heard his rage again and wondered; didn't you think my mother feared him too?

But you never asked.

Just like us, you fell in line. I see now that in a way, you were a victim too.

As a teenager, sickened by the lie I was made to live, I hung poetry on the wall, and searched for affection. I wondered who I was and how much longer I must reject the part of me that was Her.

In my silence, you never asked why. I understand now that you were afraid to know.

My father wrote your story, just like he wrote mine, once upon a time. But the truth never left me, my mother's love, crumbling beneath the force of a myth. I remember it.

I remember all that you did not want to know, all that you never asked.

An Alienated Daughter's Blog

If You See My Mother

If you see my mother today, be kind.

She has gone through the worst kind of hell you see, the unimaginable heartbreak of losing a child. Two children, actually.

In addition, she has suffered the shame and shunning that comes from people who don't understand, people who think it is her fault. People who think she must not *deserve* her children. Don't be one of those people.

If you find my mother hiding, be kind. If you notice her heart is shielded, be kind.

Know that things are not always as they seem. Know that a parent without her child may be good but now broken, and undeserving of such judgement.

You may see my mother in the grocery store, on the street, in the school or at work. You may be her friend, neighbor, brother, acquaintance. You may be her child's teacher, coach or parent of a friend.

Know that *you may not know*. You may not know the truth, her heart, the tragedy that may have unfolded. You may not know the heartbreak and the horror of what she has gone through. Know that you may not know.

Be kind.

When you see my mother, even if she has downcast eyes or meets you with silence, a protected heart, be kind.

If she is hiding or alone or hesitant to see you, *see her anyway*.

Consider that she has been broken in the cruelest possible way.

Consider that she may never heal from what has been taken from her.

She may not be able to love again with a full heart, because her heart has been shattered.

Love her anyway.

Be kind.

An Alienated Daughter's Blog

Childhood Trauma

Childhood trauma, if not healed and released, is very likely to lead to significant health issues in adulthood. It is time to call BS on the beliefs that keep us from healing, such as:
Time heals all wounds.
What doesn't kill you makes you stronger.
God doesn't give us more than we can handle.
Leave the past in the past.
The past can't hurt you anymore.
Groundbreaking research in neuroscience, psychology and medicine tells us that childhood trauma shapes our biology- our brains and our immune system- in ways that predetermine our adult health. The more adverse experiences, the higher our chances of developing heart disease, cancer, autoimmune diseases, fibromyalgia, alcoholism, depression, etc.

The Adverse Childhood Experiences quiz consists of ten questions regarding childhood traumas such as:
* Being verbally put down & humiliated
* Being emotionally or physically neglected
* Being physically or sexually abused
* Witnessing one's mother being abused
* Living w/ a parent who is depressed, mentally ill or addicted to alcohol or other substance
* Losing a parent to separation or divorce

The higher one's ACE score, the greater the risk of disease. According to research, scoring 4 or higher can shorten your life span by 20 years!

Awareness and education are the first steps along the path to healing. No one wants to live in the past, but the truth is that the past is living *within us.* Until we address our histories and then commit to healing trauma, we are essentially neglecting ourselves, mind, body, and spirit. Time does not heal all wounds. But courage does.

An Alienated Daughter's Blog

God, Are You My Mother?

My mother's loss is the soul wound that I've tried to patch up, *wanting to be whole with all my might.* Page after page, I've pieced myself back together and most of my days have been good, really good.

But the *best* day, the day that I truly felt whole, well that has taken me a long time to even contemplate writing about. I recall that day - and the days that followed- with such clarity, but what if the telling makes it less real? What if I am giving something away that was meant only for me? The *something* felt both simple and miraculous which is especially hard to describe.

Which brings to God and the day I met Him. Or Her. Or perhaps more accurately, All That Is. Creator. Higher Consciousness. I am not a particularly religious person in the traditional sense. I don't go to church. I've never read the bible. But when you think you've been broken, eventually you turn to God to fix you. I prayed, I meditated. I did God my own way, which was privately, quietly, and with my whole heart.

Then one day God showed up like a Mother. I mean she *showed up* in a very big *and* very ordinary way. I had gone to bed the night before distraught over something, the details of which are not important, but that had everything to do with thinking that *I was not yet whole.* I could not undo the past. I had all the material things I needed, and I had true love in my life. I also had my writing, my passions. But that night I still felt that gaping hole where my wound was. That night, I lost hope that I could *completely, once and for all fix myself,* so I turned it over to God. I turned my un-whole self over.

I recall that I surrendered, completely and intentionally; I am talking *Jesus take the wheel* surrender. And then I fell asleep.

The next morning, well, how can I tell you about this? How do I frame it? I am afraid of sounding like the evangelical I am not. But here it is: I was new. Real. Whole. And so very alive. I remember it all so clearly, so I will tell it clearly too.

I remember there were five states of being. Without any effort on my part, there were just these five ways of being that *took me over*. Nothing at all was new on the outside, but I was suddenly different, elevated, on the inside. And none of these simple ways of being were brand new to me per say; it's just that there was a shift, an upgrade.

Presence: I was completely in the moment. My mind was not on the past or the future. I remember the phone ringing and not wanting to answer it, because I absolutely did not want to be pulled out of the present moment. I was totally, completely, *there,* mind, body and spirit. Instead of overthinking, worrying, and analyzing, I was simply *being*. I spent much less time in my head, and more time in in my body where my heart dwelled, where my feelings could flow through me. Instead of *thinking, thinking, thinking*, I was *living*. Life was *now*.

Joy: I was completely satisfied with the moment, no matter what I was doing. Whether I was performing a chore or taking a walk, it was *joyful*. I had no craving, no desire for something different. I was *enjoying* life in the purest sense of the word.

Love: I was filled with love for myself and others. I was *overflowing* with love. I *was* love.

Self-Care: I recognized and met my own needs, moment by moment, simply, and directly. When I was hungry, I ate. When I was full, I stopped. When I was tired, I laid down. I exercised moderately and without fanfare or much planning. *I just did it.* And I accepted my body completely, knowing I was giving it whatever it needed, without obsessing or even *thinking* about it, really.

Belief: I knew that anything was possible. God was within me. My self-imposed limits vanished. I knew that the more I "let go," and allowed myself to be guided into right action, the better chance of achieving whatever I wanted.

And that is it. That is all of what I felt, and all of what I became that day that I met my highest self, or whatever you want to call it, more up close than I ever had. I was living from my Whole Self and it felt *amazing*.

It lasted a few days, or a week at most. And they were the most glorious days. But slowly, my doubt came back. My distracted mind returned. I judged again, including myself, and I neglected my own care. Bit by bit, I gave my power away without meaning to. My ego woke back up. I got busy and overwhelmed. I didn't pay attention. *I didn't check in with my Self.* I started to lose my way again.

But the biggest gift from my "moment in the light" is that I know what to strive for now: *To be more present, to find joy in my life every single day, to love and care for myself and to find the best in others. To believe that all of this is possible. Every. Single. Day.* To be in that light was such a feeling, a consciousness, and honestly felt like the most important goal I could ever have. It *is* my most important goal now; to live consciously, awake, aligned.

I aim to feel this way every day now, to get there with my choices, sometimes the simplest of ones.

I often fall short, but God meets me in the middle.

I am whole, just like you are. I was all along. I'd just forgotten.

An Alienated Daughter's Blog

A Message From Your Alienated Child

I am three years old. You are no longer in our home and my world is shattered. I saw Daddy's anger toward you and I will be careful not to make him angry at me too.

I am four years old and my visits with you are dwindling. Please do not give up your rights. Take what action you can, whatever action is right and necessary. Find those who can help you. Find those who will hold you up, because my world depends upon you not giving up. Do not believe Daddy when he says I am better off without you. I need you to know that is a lie.

I am five years old and you dare to show up on my birthday, to deliver a gift. I want you to know that I am so glad you are there, but I am afraid to say so. I see how agitated Daddy is by your presence. I want to tell you, beg you, to please keep coming back. But I cannot say what I need you to know.

My sister sounds angry at you and tells you not to come back. She says we have a new mother and we don't need you anymore. She doesn't mean it. She will regret that moment in years to come and she will suffer from thinking they were *her* words. I will regret that you believed her.

I am eight years old. You have been erased from my life. My sister and I whisper about you in our bedroom at night, in the dark. We don't dare speak your name, so we call you You-Know-Who. We remember you. Signs of you, some memories, a hidden photograph, they let us know you are real. They ignite something in me, too wounded to dwell in, but at the same time a place of truth and power that I will have access to someday.

I am ten years old. If you somehow managed to contact me now, I would probably not respond. It would terrify me to respond. But without a doubt, I would remember your efforts. I would know that you wanted me. I would know that you tried. This would make me want to find you again when I was ready.

I am fifteen. My sister and I sneak away to visit you. Of course, we don't tell our father. I am numb and my sister is still angry at you, questioning you. Where were you? Why did you have that affair that made our father throw you out? How dare you? Why didn't you come looking for us later?

I am numb, mute, perhaps in shock at seeing you again. You cry and say you love us, have always loved us. I don't fully take in your words even though they are the ones I need to hear. My wounded teenage heart needs to be reminded of what I knew as a baby, as a toddler, as a three-year-old: that you love me. You've had obstacles, huge obstacles in the way, but I need to know that indifference was not one of them.

I am sixteen. I don't know who I am. I have been taught to deny the part of me that came from you. I am trying to fill the void where you were supposed to be. I think I can do this with boys, with teenage affairs, with affection from whoever will offer it to me. The void is deep and will need to be healed with truth, with love, with understanding. I don't know this yet though, so I just keep trying to fill it with things that aren't good for me.

I am eighteen. I am free to contact you or visit you, but I am still very much afraid of displeasing my father. I need you to be strong and healthy and to remind me, somehow, that you are waiting. I have wandered so far from that place in my heart that holds us together. It will take patience and persistence on your part. I need to see that you love yourself, so that I can allow myself to love you too.

I am twenty-four. I will want to hear your story. I *need* to hear your story. And I will believe you. I am not sure what to do with this yet, how to let you into my life. I will have to figure this out. I am angry that *you* weren't able to stand up to my father and therefore I was robbed of a mother. I am angry at my father but still afraid to tell him so, to face him with my truth. This will take time and clumsy attempts, but I hope I will figure it out.

I am every age. Know that you can reach me and hold me in your mind's eye. Believe that there is some purpose to this mess and that we will both be okay. I will find my way back to you. It may be when I remember I am your daughter or it may be when I find that bigger part of me, the self who is neither my father's daughter nor my mother's daughter, nor a victim; the Self that is whole and was never lost, never abandoned, never hurt. This could be a long, slow process, or it could happen in a moment, in a word I hear, in a prayer I feel, coming from you.

An Alienated Daughter's Blog

The Stories We Tell

Pat Conroy's *The Great Santini* is fiction that reads like memoir. Like a lot of fiction, the author's real experiences are on the page. Calling it fiction allowed his father, the tyrant in the story, to temporarily deny its truth. Conroy offers up his angst to the page, one scene at a time. His words do not convey self-pity, but rather a detached yet descriptive unfolding of his history. In the end, his father owned up to the truths in the book, and the two men redeemed their relationship.

I considered writing my book as fiction, but have made my choice to call it what it is, a memoir. Still, I definitely understand Conroy's choice. To call a true story fiction is an act of self-protection, or maybe of protection of others as well, to offer them up the possibility that *it was all made up. It's just a tale, something from nothing, no big deal, we can all go home now.* I do see the appeal in that.

Secrets and suffering are ingredients of nearly every memoir. Mine is no exception.

The absence of truth is usually a lie, and in the case of family tragedy, pretending to the outside world that all is well leads the most introspective amongst us to take notes, both literally and metaphorically speaking. My memoir is the accumulation of all my mental notes. They started when I was four.

I know something of that need to bring "the thing" to light by way of the written word. The desire is compelling, and almost beyond choice. Most memoirists have suffered greatly before they craft their story for the public. But many suffer even more afterwards, or so I hear. That part is scary and surely tests the desire to offer the story up to the world.

From the outside, my family was ordinary by many people's standards. But the loss of my mother was extraordinary and therefore I must write it.

As I am nearing the end of it, I imagine my father's response to my words. He somehow had convinced himself that erasing my mother was excusable, even necessary. To face these pages from the lens of my loss would not sit well with him. But it is also quite possible that he will never read it.

I understand that - the not wanting to read it - or even needing to deny that it is written. I empathize with the pain of being exposed, and the vulnerability. But I can no longer take on his feelings as my responsibility. Nor is it anyone's job to tend to mine. I've got this now.

And in the depths of my soul, I know that we are all vulnerable. My father has been my teacher and the lessons have been hard, really hard. But I believe in something of a soul agreement, chosen before we even come here to this this side of the veil. It helps to believe that I actually chose my particular lessons, and that I needed my father to help carry them out. We all have our lessons, and my story just happens to contain mine.

My aim is truth and courage, and forgiveness too.

An Alienated Daughter's Blog

Relevance

In the midst of a pandemic, I get my first book contract and let the cognitive dissonance settle in. I am elated! It is meaningless! By the time the book is published, will the words I've written even matter? In a world full of sickness and chaos, is art even relevant?

My husband and I go away to celebrate our 33rd anniversary. He is reluctant in these times, but I've found us a private spot on Cape Cod, we pack a bag, some food, and we go. On the drive down I am describing the adorable guest house I have secured for us. I am happy to escape the everydayness of our lives, the news, the impertinence of my writing.

It is called the Sweetest Little Suite, I tell him.

It has probably been renamed The Covid Cabin, he quips.

Don't make me laugh, I say. *There is nowhere to pee.*

I know the state of the country, the *world* for God's sake, is not funny right now. It is dark and uncertain, but we need to laugh when we can because the crying will come too, if not for ourselves, for others.

It is freakishly warm for the middle of November, but we don't see anyone else at the seashore except for maybe a few people sitting so far down the beach they are like large grains of sand, their movement almost imperceptible.

It starts off as a dare, me tempting my husband to jump into the crashing waves, and it ends with both of us stripping down, running into the ocean, going under. He disappears first and when he pops up he is shouting for me to hurry before the next wave drags me violently across the sand. Shrieking, I dive in, my timing more a reflex of panic than any kind of strategy.

When you've been married this long, there aren't many firsts you haven't met; first home, first child, first move, job loss, illness. We've had them all. But this- today- skinny-dipping in the ocean in the middle of fall — for our November anniversary — this is a new first.

I emerge from the cold, invigorated. The sun warms my skin as it creates glitter across the water. The reflection is spectacular; there is so much light. I am insignificant, but at the same time connected to the brilliance of God's creativity.

Fully present, mind and body in harmony, I take it all in. I see and feel the ocean, the world, as the most amazing work of art.

In this moment, the art is everything.

APPENDIX B
Recommended Reading

An Attachment-Based Model of Parental Alienation: Foundations
by Dr. Craig Childress (2015, Oaksong Press)

Splitting
by Bill Eddy (2021, Tantor Audio

Divorce Poison
by Dr. Richard Warshak (2015, Tantor Audio)

Why Does He Do That? Inside the Minds of Angry and Controlling Men
by Lundy Bancroftt (2003, Berkley Books)

Childhood Disrupted: How Your Biography Becomes Your Biology and How You Can Heal
by Donna Jackson Nakazawa (2016, Atria Books)

Running on Empty
by Jonice Webb, PhD (2012, Morgan James Publishing)

The Body Keeps the Score
by Bessel van der Kolk (2015, Penguin Publishing Group)

Half the Child
A novel by William J. McGee (2018, McGee)

AUTHOR'S NOTE

It has taken several years for me to write this memoir, but in a way, I have been writing it my whole life. I am deeply grateful to the readers who have encouraged me along the way, proving to me that my story has a deeper purpose than just my own account; you have given me the courage and the will to keep putting words on the page. It is my hope and my intention that this book lands in the hands of those who benefit from knowing my story, who will glean some insight or understanding that will help them along their own journeys.

In writing this memoir, I drew from memory, letters and emails, as well as many conversations over the span of five decades. I have remained true to my recollection of all events. Some names have been changed.

www.ingramcontent.com/pod-product-compliance
Lightning Source LLC
Chambersburg PA
CBHW031323160426

43196CB00007B/637